Thomas Holmes

Light in Dark Places

Theological Nuts, Philosophically Cracked, on the Rock of the Scriptures, with the

Hammer of Common Sense

Thomas Holmes

Light in Dark Places
Theological Nuts, Philosophically Cracked, on the Rock of the Scriptures, with the Hammer of Common Sense

ISBN/EAN: 9783337270360

Printed in Europe, USA, Canada, Australia, Japan

Cover: Foto ©Lupo / pixelio.de

More available books at **www.hansebooks.com**

BORN NOV. 24, 1817.   TAKEN NOV. 24, 1897.

Thomas Holmes.

LIGHT IN DARK PLACES

Theological Nuts, Philosophically Cracked, on the Rock
of the Scriptures, with the Hammer
of Common Sense

BY

Rev. Thomas Holmes, D. D.

Prove all things, hold fast that which is good.—I Thess. v. 21.

ANN ARBOR, MICH.:
THE INLAND PRESS
1898.

INTRODUCTION.

Every doctrine of a philosophical nature is pronounced true or false as it agrees or disagrees with a theory, hypothecated as a radical fact, according to which all phenomena pertaining to said theory are supposed to be explicable. The Ptolemaic system of astronomy was based upon the theory that the earth is the center of the universe, around which all celestial bodies revolve. Although this theory was known to be defective, in that certain phenomena could not be accounted for on that hypothesis, yet it could not be refuted until a theory was found that would furnish a rational and satisfactory explanation of all such phenomena. This the Copernican system finally accomplished; but it required the lapse of a century, and the passing away of three generations of Ptolemaic philosophers, before its triumph was complete.

Something very similar has also transpired in the theological world. The theory of the absolute, arbitrary, irresponsible Sovereignty of God, actuated by supreme devotion to his own glory, according to which, as elaborated by John Calvin, God foreordained whatsoever comes to pass, and predestinated, from eternity, the salvation of a portion of our race and the damnation of another portion, individually, notwithstanding the shocking conclusions to which it logically led, has prevailed and been regarded as irrefutable for three hundred years, for the want of the careful working out of a better theory. In the following lectures the author believes he has thrown light upon many dark, mysterious, unsettled questions, through the application of the philosophy of Moral Agency.

When Galileo announced to an astonished world that Jupiter had four moons, and his statement was disputed with great vehemence by others, because they could not see them, his unanswerable reply was, "Look through my telescope." In leaving this little volume behind me, as I step off "the stage of action," I want to make the same request. Let not the reader hastily pronounce the doctrines false that are taught in the following pages, because they do not all agree with popular opinions, with the teaching of some other author, or with his own ideas respecting them. Orthodoxy is progressive. Truths plainly taught in the Scriptures may yet remain undiscovered, for lack of the lens that is adapted to find them.

The churches of two hundred years ago would not have received as private members, much less as pastors and theological teachers, the most distinguished theologians and preachers of the present day. The fact that some of the views here presented are new, and differ from doctrines the reader has been taught, lacks a great deal of being evidence that they are false. Satellites had revolved in their orbits around Jupiter for untold ages before Galileo published the fact on this planet; and there are, undoubtedly, satellite truths revolving around the fundamental doctrines of the gospel, clearly revealed in the Word of God, yet undiscovered.

The topics here discussed furnish an inviting field for original investigation; because the key that unlocks their mysteries, the light that reveals their nature and logical connections, is now better understood, more clearly seen, than ever before since the world began. That light is acquaintance with the nature and philosophy of Moral Agency, and its practical bearings upon the relations of man to his God and to his fellow men.

These lectures deal mostly with disputed questions, and questions that are regarded, by many at least, as beyond the reach of human investigation. The author has no expectation that his views will receive the immediate assent of all his readers; nor that all his views will receive the immediate assent of any one of them. He hopes, however, when he does not convince, to awaken thought and investigation that will ultimately lead to progress along all these lines.

Whatever may be found herein that seems to the reader heretical will not be the result of reckless disregard of the Scriptures of divine truth; nor of a determination to make out a case or carry a point, regardless of evidence, or of the opinions of others; nor of the legitimate effect of the doctrines taught upon Christian faith, and upon the Christian lives of those who may believe them. We fully believe that faith in the doctrines here taught will result in a far more intelligent, and for that reason in a far more consistent, successful and acceptable Christian life than can possibly result from belief of the errors here refuted.

Of all conceivable attitudes of the human mind towards the facts, realities, conditions, circumstances, relations, obligations, and final awards of a human life, that which is most momentously important is a willingness, an earnest and intense desire and determination, to know the truth, the exact truth, and nothing but the truth, in regard to everything that has a bearing upon the welfare of the soul, both in this life and in the life to come. Error is no advantage to any one. Deception, whether self-imposed or practiced upon us by another, has no other than evil tendencies. Truth may not always be agreeable to us; may not always flatter our hopes or encourage our desires and wishes, but it is always the best for us in the end, the very thing we need to know, to accept, to believe, to act upon.

In investigating the questions discussed in this volume, we have endeavored to look at them from this standpoint, and from this standpoint we ask our readers to look at them. The views here presented are the result of more than three score years of study; nearly all of which was intended to be original investigation. An unbiased attitude of mind, in matters that have been subjects of thought and discussion for ages, may possibly be unattainable, but it surely may be approached.

A heart thoroughly consecrated to truth, not its apprehension only but its practice; a persistent purpose to embrace in premises every fact and circumstance obtainable, that has a bearing upon the conclusion sought, with large opportunities for obtaining such facts; an honest and resolute determination to hold every opinion previously formed subject to such modification as new light, from any source, may demand; long and patient labor, with frequent re-examination of work already performed; earnest and constant prayer for divine illumination; the whole prompted by at least a hope that the conclusions arrived at may stand for truth during ages yet to come; are elements and necessary conditions of independent investigation. How far these have had sway in the mind and heart and labor of the author final results will determine.

As postulates of procedure, the author has had frequent recourse to the following:

1. Nothing should be rejected because it is old, nor received because it is new; neither should any doctrine be regarded as unalterable because it is old, nor rejected because it is new. While the fact that a doctrine has for ages been regarded as established is *prima facie* evidence of its truth, every doctrine, old or new, must yield the ground, when the evidence in its favor is overweighed by reliable evidence against it.

2. Theorems in ethics and theology, in the light shed upon them by the nature and philosophy of moral agency, are as demonstrable as theorems in geometry.

3. There is not a truth in the universe, whether it relates to Creator or creature, that God is not willing we should know, if we will find it, and bring it to the light. Hence there is nothing too sacred for the most free and searching investigation. We should investigate all truth reverently, but should not let undue reverence hinder thoroughness. Above all things, we need have no fear nor hesitation in inquiring into the nature, essence, constitution, attributes, motives and methods of the Deity. There is nothing about God that he is unwilling we should know; and the more we know about him the more we shall revere him, the more perfectly shall we love him, and the more intelligently and acceptably shall we be able to serve him.

4. No statement can be true that diametrically contradicts reason and our knowledge of positive facts.

Respecting the heresies my readers will think they find here, I want to say a few words. I am as well aware as any of my readers can be that, measured by the accepted standards of "orthodoxy," many of the conclusions here stated with great positiveness must be pronounced erroneous; some of them perhaps dangerous.

This fact has been the greatest stumbling block in the way of publishing the book. The approbation of others is very pleasant to me. I never realized the meaning of what has been called "the courage of conviction," until I faced seriously the question, Shall I give to the world the candid, honest, solemn conclusions at which I have arrived? I am sure that no one who has never been brought face to face with such a question has any idea of the courage required to be true to God, true to conviction, true to the world, in the full consciousness of the possibility, perhaps the certainty, that dear and valued friends will cry out, "Away with him! Crucify him!"

While some of the nuts that we believe we have successfully cracked have been enveloped in a very thin shell, others have been incased in a very strange, unreasoning and unreasonable faith, or, more truly, appearance of faith—faith falsely so called —that has for ages prevented the least approach to a careful, thorough investigation. As such doctrines are held in an unreasoning, unquestioning state of mind, any proposal to inquire into the soundness of the foundation upon which they rest is repelled at once, and refused consideration. By such persons many doctrines are declared to be too mysterious for comprehension, and must be taken on the *ipse dixit* of others who have enveloped them in mystery, but declared them to be true.

This idea we have rejected entirely. We know of no mysteries, connected with God's methods of redeeming the fallen race of man, that may not be inquired into with the confident expectation of finding them conceivable and reasonable. We admit that many things, facts that are to be believed, are of so high a grade of wisdom that we may not, in our present state of knowledge, or more properly ignorance, fathom and comprehend their philosophy; but we maintain, and work upon the hypothesis, that nothing can be true that squarely and positively contradicts our reason. He who made truth that pertains to his creatures has given those to whom it pertains reason to apprehend it.

We accept willingly a paradox. We like to study a paradox. Its apparent contradiction contains a truth, and is a most impressive method of teaching it. Such a nut must necessarily require a certain degree of intelligence to crack it, in some cases more than in others, but it may be cracked, and its meat will be a luxury; its reasonableness will be clear and impressive. This is very different from an absurdity that squarely and positively contradicts reason, ignores well-known and universal facts, and defies the affirmations of common sense.

It is useless to wrap such statements in "mystery," and declare them to be incomprehensible to finite minds, but still truths that must be believed, the doubting of which should be branded as heresy. He who thus defies the demands of Christian charitableness is himself the worst of heretics. It is far worse to be disloyal to love than to dogma. Dogma may be false, but love is always true. "Now abideth faith, hope, love, these three; but the greatest of these is love."

Some may inquire why I have not, in

formal statement, arraigned the errors that stand over against the truths here presented. My reply is, My object is not controversy. I do not believe the controversial method of handling religious questions, or any other questions, to be the best. The moment you arraign a supposed error, in that manner, you put its advocates upon its defense; and soon the attitude of the parties is not that of mutual inquest for truth, but which shall down his antagonist, whether by fair means or foul.

My purpose is, if possible, to secure a candid hearing, by diverting the attention of an opponent from his fortifications, and, by a flag of truce, lure him into the open field, where we may confer together, not in a warlike but in a peaceable and reasonable manner. If I succeed in presenting my view of the question in a clear, convincing, unanswerable manner, any candid reader will probably see, by looking through my telescope, objects that he cannot find in the one he has been using, and rejoice in the revelation of truth not previously apprehended.

When you wish to light up a dark room, carry in a light, and the darkness will flee away, without any argument, persuasion, threat or fight for possession. Error is darkness, truth is light. Let in the light, and there will be no darkness to fight.

Of my critics I want to ask this favor. Lay aside, while reading this book, the glass through which you are accustomed to look at the questions here discussed, and look through my telescope; consider them in the light in which I have presented them. "Prove all things, hold fast that which is good." If you and I differ, one of us must be wrong. We may both be wrong, but it is impossible that we should both be right. If we carefully compare views, we may discover where the error lies, and both find the truth. There is not a doctrine advanced, in the entire book, that the author will not renounce, if greater weight of truth and reason can be found against it than for it. Has the reader the moral courage to take the same attitude? If so, give us your hand. It is a bargain. I will look through your telescope, if you will look through mine. "Come and let us reason together."

With these words of introduction and

explanation, we lay our offering upon the altar of free, untrammeled inquiry, with the earnest prayer and hope that it may be accepted of God, receive his benediction wherever it may find a reader, and be helpful to all who are earnest seekers after truth.

CHELSEA, MICH., January, 1898.

CONTENTS.

LECTURE I.
MORAL AGENCY.

	PAGE.
Conditions of—	
1. Intelligence	1
2. Free will	2
3. Opportunity to make a choice	5
Such was the tree of forbidden fruit	6
This story veritable history	9
Questions answered	11

LECTURE II.
SOUL, BODY, AND SPIRIT.

Confusion of ideas respecting	16
Jews and Christian fathers, trichotomists	17
What is the Soul?	19
Suggestion to psychologists	21
What is the body? What are its uses?	23
What is the spirit?	24
It is a human spirit	25
It is the gift of God	26
Uses of the spirit	27
The spiritual body	29
The man complete	30
Thus constituted, must be a moral agent	32
Brutes di-chotomous, cannot be moral agents	33
Certain passages of Scripture	35

LECTURE III.
THE FALL.

Moral condition in which Adam and Eve were created	38
Temptation necessary	40
The transgression	42
Physical death not the result of sin	44
"Dust thou art and unto dust shalt thou return" was no part of the curse	47

LECTURE IV.
LAW.

Physical laws	51
Ceremonial laws	61
Moral laws	64
Not enactments of a sovereign	65
Arise from relations. God subject to them as well as men	66
Law makers should understand this	70
The ten commandments	72
The fourth commandment	73
Fallacy of sabbatarians	76
Reasons and authority for the change	77

LECTURE V.
PENALTIES.

Governments exist for the benefit of the governed	82
Penalties of divine law not punitive	83
Divine idea of punishment disciplinary	84
Treatment of incorrigible offenders	86
No treatment of sinners inconsistent with love	88

LECTURE VI.
THE ATONEMENT.

The word defined	90
Parties to be reconciled	91
Sin; its misery and bondage. This is hell	92
Moral agency not destroyed by the bondage of sin	92
Seventh chapter of Romans not Christian experience	93
Jesus, the Christ, comes to deliver	96
Justice and Mercy not antagonistic	96
God's purpose is to secure, by merciful means, the ends demanded by justice	98
The exact situation described	100
When Justice and Mercy are both satisfied, nothing more is necessary	102
How did Jesus, the son of man, effect this?	104
The incorrigible not benefitted by the atonement	107
Love more potent than dread of punishment to secure loyalty	108
Grateful loyalty more potent than the strongest resolutions to resist temptation	111
A better end reached than justice ever dreamed of	112
The lost compelled to acknowledge the justice of their condemnation	112
Merciful agencies move the sinner to penitence, which punishment never does	113
These points gained, pardon is safe	114
Multitudes now saved, when all would have been lost	115
The plan of salvation not an after-thought	116

Jesus' sacrifice and suffering voluntary.... 117
That no sacrifice was necessary, a fallacy.. 119
Remarks................................. 121

LECTURE VII.
REGENERATION—CONVERSION.

These words not synonymous............. 129
Moral condition of the unregenerate...... 131
No happiness in this condition........... 135
The steps of this progressive change: viz.,
 the begetting of a new life by the Spirit,
 heeding the call, penitence, repentance,
 prayer for pardon, pardon, faith, witness of the Spirit, are treated in their
 order........................137 to 155

LECTURE VIII.
ANGELS.

Who are the angels?..................... 156
Are they moral agents?.................. 158
Some of them sinned and became demons 160
Personality of the devil................. 166
Who made the devil? A silly question.... 170
Why are demons allowed to tempt us?.... 173

LECTURE IX.
THE GODHEAD.

The word Godhead suggests, and the word
 Elohim expresses plurality of persons.. 178
The first person is the Infinite ONE...... 179
His necessary attributes................. 182
His moral attributes..................... 191
Is God a moral agent?................... 193
The Executive Deity—the Word—the Son 202

The second person in the Godhead...... 204
A distinct, self-conscious person.......... 205
Esposition of John 1:1, The Word was
    God.............................. 206
The Holy Spirit—His personality......... 225
Uses of the phrase Holy Spirit........... 229
Whence does the Holy Spirit "proceed?".. 241
Is the Holy Spirit a third person in the
    Godhead?.......................... 246
Objections answered..................... 252

LECTURE X.

ETERNAL PUNISHMENT.

An important error disposed of.......... 256
The sin against the Holy Spirit.......... 259
Eternal punishment means eternal sin.... 260
Moral agency shows its possibility....... 261
Jesus taught its certainty............... 263
Same result reached by another argument.. 265
Who are the lost?....................... 267
This eternal doom self-inflicted.......... 270

LECTURE XI.

FUTURE PROBATION.

Eternal sin means eternal moral agency... 272
This question of no significance to those
    who have made their choice.......... 273
Classes to which this question pertains.... 274
To what source shall we look for light?... 275
Moral agency means probation; hence,
    every moral agent, good or bad, will be
    eternally on probation............... 281
This fact assures moral stability......... 283

ERRATA.

Page 61.—Change 2 to II.
Page 64.—Change 3 to III.

LECTURE I.

MORAL AGENCY.

Many have confused ideas on the subject of moral agency, because they suppose an agent to be one who transacts business for another, and that the employer is responsible for the acts of the agent. This is not the primary use of the word. The Standard Dictionary defines thus:—"Agent. 1. One who or that which acts or has the power to act; an active power or efficient cause of any thing. 2. One who or that which acts for another." In speaking of a moral agent, the word is always used in its primary sense.

A moral agent is a voluntary actor, whose acts may have moral character; that is, may be right or wrong. This will be more clearly understood as we proceed to consider

THE CONDITIONS OF MORAL AGENCY.

1. An indispensable condition of moral agency is a kind and degree of intelligence that will enable its possessor to receive in-

struction by precept. He must understand, from preceptive instruction, what to do, why he should do it, and that consequences depend upon obedience or disobedience. Brutes learn only from experience; hence moral agency is to them impossible. Not to be able to understand the import of a command, and the nature of an obligation, until the consequences of obedience or disobedience are learned from experience, would be an anomaly and absurdity in morals.

The intelligence of a moral agent must also be sufficient to enable him to reason *a priori*. The connection between cause and effect must be obvious to him, and hence the nature, importance and sacredness of an obligation will be apprehended through a rational perception, and his act of obedience or disobedience will be intentional, in consideration of or in disobedience to his sense of obligation, as apprehended by his intelligence.

2. Another indispensable condition of moral agency is what is called the Free Will. By free will is meant will acting in the presence of an alternative—the soul so situated

that it can choose this or that. Two ways, or more, are open before it; either, or any one, of which it can enter or refuse to enter. This is also called Will in Liberty; because the will is at liberty to make choice of either of two, or any one of several, objects or courses of conduct. The Free Will, Will in Liberty, resembles very closely a judge, considering a case as presented by contending advocates. Each advocate pleads his case, giving his reasons why decision should be rendered in his favor, and the judge decides in favor of one as against the others.

In making its choices, the will is absolutely, unqualifiedly self-determining. It is defiant of any authority, human or divine, or any coercive influence that can be brought upon it. It can be influenced by reason, if it choose to listen to reason; but in spite of all the demands of reason that which is unreasonable may be chosen. It matters not what direful consequences may impend; how dreadful to the thought, how painful to the feelings, how torturing to the flesh, how maddening to the conscience; the will; that is, the soul in the exercise of its choice, may still maintain an attitude of resistance, defiance, insubordination. On the other hand, the will is just as capable, just as independent, just as potential, in its choice of that which is right, when it so determines. The world, the flesh and the devil, all the hosts and powers of darkness, are impotent to compel its assent to that which is wrong. The will of a moral agent cannot be coerced. The brute will must yield to the demands of the flesh; the human will may refuse obedience to the demands both of the flesh and of the spirit, even the Spirit of God. Few people seem to have any conception of this wonderful sovereignty of the will. In the freedom of its action, in its choices, it is as independent of the will of God, as the will of God is independent of the will of man. This will in liberty, this power of unrestrained, uncoerced, independent choice, is the most wonderful of all the creations of the Infinite One, of which we have any knowledge. This unlimited sovereignty of choice is the necessary, the unalterable condition, the constitutional basis, of every act that has moral character. For such acts, and such only, the actor, the agent, is responsible and accountable. He who is thus endowed, and he only, is a moral agent. This peculiarity of man, this capacity for moral agency, is "the image of God" in which he was created.

The positive, and the only positive, proof of this freedom, this sovereignty, is consciousness. There is not a moral agent in the universe, who has not the consciousness that he possesses the power to thus make his own choices, irrespective of the commands, the wishes, even the persuasions, of any other person in the universe or of all others united.

3. The third condition of moral agency, or more properly of a moral act, is opportunity to make a choice; that is, the presence of an alternative. Whatever may be the degree of intelligence with which the Creator has endowed the creature, unless an alternative of action is present, no act that the creature can perform can have moral character. Such opportunities are present, whenever intelligent beings are in such circumstances as create an obligation

to pursue a given course of conduct. Only in such circumstances has the free will opportunity to make a choice for which it alone —that is, the soul thus exercising choice— is responsible. The necessary alternative is found in these circumstances. They constitute the opportunity.

Such opportunities are all comprised in one's duties to God, to other intelligences human or angelic, to any sentient creature, and to himself. His loyalty to God, to righteousness, to self, is thus tested; and his loyalty or disloyalty is made manifest. Men do not even know themselves until thus tested; much less are they known to others.

The tree of forbidden fruit, mentioned in Gen. 2: 16, 17, is intended to illustrate both the fact and the nature of such opportunities. God has often been blamed for placing that temptation before our innocent first parents. Men say, "Why did God place a tree in the garden of Eden, the fruit of which should be forbidden? Manifestly our parents were happy, until they partook of that fruit. Why not let them continue happy? Does not this act, if we give credence to the story, directly and positively antagonize the oft asserted claim that God is infinitely wise and benevolent? Surely this must have been a blunder that compromises his wisdom, or an act of malevolence that contradicts his goodness."

Thus "bold, bad men" question the claims of Christianity, in regard to this act of Providence; while others, whose confidence in God is so firm and unshaken that they avow faith in what seems to them to contradict reason, observation and experience, are quite unable to reconcile the paradox. To both these classes let me say, All the mysteries of this extraordinary transaction are easily solved in the light of the nature and principles of moral agency.

This tree of forbidden fruit furnished the opportunity for our first parents to prove their loyalty to their Creator and Sovereign; their worthiness of the exalted position they occupied in the creation; and also to greatly increase their own happiness. The question to be tested was whether they would obey God or disobey him. Obedience would have made them holy, and brought to their consciousness his approving smile, which would have been life to them. . "Thy favor is life." The blissful satisfaction that results from doing right would have been theirs. Instead of this, they disobeyed, and found out immediately that "the wages of sin is death," just as God had predicted. The serpent had assured them positively, "Thou shalt not surely die"; but the act was displeasing to God, they lost his favor, they were dead.

This act of disobedience was entirely voluntary, their own act. No one could be blamed for it but themselves. The tempter was responsible for the lie he told, and for soliciting them to disobey; but the act of transgression was theirs. This is accountability. Hence comes character. Without this test (or some other) to do wrong, to disobey, moral character would have been impossible. Note well, however, any one of ten thousand other tests would have answered the same purpose; and would, undoubtedly, have been followed by the same result. Manifestly God chose this because the nature of the whole transaction could be easily understood and comprehended by the human mind, even in the infancy of our race.

If asked if I believe the account of the temptation and fall, as given in the third chapter of Genesis, to be veritable history, I answer, Certainly. The questioning of the reliability of the account given us of this transaction is one of the many instances of inexcusable ignorance, that result from thoughtlessness and neglect to exercise common sense. The record of the transaction is given to reveal to the race two facts, that it is of the greatest importance to them to understand. These are the nature of an obligation, and the freedom of a moral agent to obey or disobey. These are the most important facts. Of minor importance is the fact that our first parents, like all their posterity, fell into sin. Is it not most reasonable to suppose that the facts in the case would be given to the world just as they occurred? What would be gained by giving a fictitious account of the event instead of a true one? Of the ten thousand tests possible, only one was necessary to test the point in question. What reason can any one give for supposing that the method actually employed was suppressed, and a fiction substituted? Is that like God? How could a falsehood serve a better purpose than the truth? What would be gained by recording a lie in order to teach an important principle of morals? Would it not be a queer example of the wisdom of the Sovereign ruler to bring so great and important an event about in such a manner that it became necessary to hide the facts in the case, and reveal the nature of the transaction by means of a falsehood? How much would that lack of doing evil that good might come? Are not facts better adapted to teach morals than fables?

Let us also bear in mind the well known fact that opportunity, as a condition to moral agency, is just as essential and just as omnipresent in the case of every son and daughter of Adam as it was in his case. Nor is forbidden fruit presented only at the commencement of responsibility. Trees of forbidden fruit, speaking now figuratively, are standing not only in every man's garden of

Eden, but on either side of the pathway of life, all the way from the cradle to the grave. These are constant tests of loyalty to God, to our fellow men, to ourselves; and the choices we make, when the opportunities are before us, will determine our character and our destiny.

A question is often asked that, although indirectly answered already, should, perhaps receive a little more attention. "If there must be opportunity to sin, why did not God make man so that he could not sin?" The only meaning this question can have, if it has any meaning at all, is, Why did not God make another order of brutes, instead of making a creature that is capable of possessing moral character, a creature that is responsible for his conduct, in short, a moral agent? The probability is that God had created all the brutes he wanted. How would it do to suggest that, knowing the end from the beginning, God saw that man would be quite ready enough to make a brute of himself? Since ability to sin is just as essential to a moral agent as opportunity to sin, he must either endow him with the power to sin, that is with a free will, or not make him a moral agent. On this very ground we assert the sovereignty of the human will over its choices, and the impossibility of its coercion. The moment the will of any intelligent being should be coerced, overpowered, so that it should not enjoy absolute freedom of choice, moral agency, and consequently accountability, would cease, and only a brute would be found, where a moral agent had been and should be.

Another question, and one of no little importance, well deserving careful attention, is, "Did the Creator know, when he created man, that he would sin? If he was aware of that dreadful fact, involving, possibly, the eternal despair of multitudes of deathless souls, what can justify him in giving existence to our race?"

To this question I answer, Most assuredly God knew, when he created man, that he would sin. Omniscience is one of his necessary attributes. Were it otherwise, he would be finite, and like other finite beings, would know nothing he did not learn. He could forecast nothing, only as the probable results of causes, with the existence of which, and with the laws of whose operation, he was already acquainted, having previously learned them; and such forecast, like the presience of man, would be very limited. Such a being would hardly be sufficient for the planning and construction of a universe like this, in which we have our being, and of which we form a part.

As to his justification, in giving existence to our race, under such fearful possibilities and certainties, this is found in the very fact that he is infinitely wise and good. Like all moral agents, God is under obligation to himself, as well as to his intelligent creatures, to seek the highest good of the greatest number. He must seek the greatest aggregation of well-being. The good of being is the motive of all his works, of all his requirements, and of all his dealings with his intelligent creatures. Because it was apparent to his infinite foresight that more good than evil would result from the creation of moral agents, he created them.

Much as we lack of the infinite benevolence that moved him to the vast undertaking, there is not one of us who would not do the same, under the same circumstances; if we had the same foresight and the same ability. Suppose the entire list of inventors, from the Marquis of Worcester to Robert Fulton, who were instrumental in the discovery and successful working of steam-power, could have foreseen all the terrible, shocking, heart rending, agonizing, indescribable accidents, by land and by sea, that would inevitably result from their experiments; and at the same time, could have had also the companion vision of all the benefits that the world would realize from their discoveries and devices, would any one justify them, had they been deterred by the grief and suffering that would result, and suppressed the great and beneficent improvements, that were brought into use by their agency; and left the world destitute of all their advantages, as we enjoy them to-day? If no moral agents had been created, brute satisfaction, simply sensuous gratification, would have been the highest enjoyment known in the whole range of sensuous creatures.

Keep ever in mind that a moral agent who can not sin is an impossibility. Thus we see not only that the wisdom and goodness of God, in creating man a moral agent, are vindicated, but that he himself would have been censurable in the highest degree; condemned, an infinite sinner, if he had not made man just as he has. We also see that the planting of the tree of forbidden fruit was one of the indispensable features of his wise and wondrous plan. Men do not "fall upward" when they fall into sin; but every opportunity to sin is also an opportunity to show their loyalty to God, and to attain a standard of virtue and holiness that can be attained only in the face of such opportunity. Ability and opportunity to sin are the indispensible conditions of holiness.

LECTURE II.

SOUL, BODY AND SPIRIT.

These words are often used in the scriptures; sometimes together, sometimes separately. In Heb. 4:12, we read of "the dividing asunder of soul and spirit," and in 1 Thess. 5:23 we read, "I pray God your whole spirit and soul and body be preserved blameless." Who has not paused, after reading these passages, and asked himself, Do these three words—soul, body, spirit—include all there is in the essence of man? and does each word both fully express its own concept, and completely exclude the concept of each and both the other words? If such is the fact, if each of these words is thus inclusive and thus exclusive, great confusion respecting the boundaries that limit the scope and realm of each exists to-day. If it is not the fact, why should their usage be characterized by a discrimination so manifest and so carefully observed throughout the word of God? In common usage, to-day, no distinction or discrimination whatever is made in the use of the words soul and spirit. Learned preachers, theological professors, commentators and common people, use these words as though they were perfect synonyms. In the word of God this is not the case. Throughout the entire scriptures we believe there is no instance, when rationally interpreted, in which these two words are used interchangeably. The word soul is never used to name the spirit; and the word spirit is never used to name the soul. The truth is they are separate parts of the man, as distinct and unlike as are the soul and the body.

The Jews held well defined ideas as to the existence of a tripartite nature in man; but precisely what psychological facts and functions were attributed to soul and spirit separately I have been unable to ascertain. Josephus (Ant. I. 1, 2) affirms that Moses says, "God took dust from the ground and formed man, and inserted in him a spirit and a soul." The early Christian Fathers; Justin Martyr, Clement, Origen and others, were clear-cut trichotomists; but the farther down the stream of time we come, the more turbid we find its waters upon this subject.

Commentators, essayists, preachers and exegetes of every class have treated the subject, some more intelligently and profoundly than others, but among them all no one has given a definition clearly discriminating between the soul and the spirit. So far as distinction is attempted, the soul is supposed by some to be the seat of the affections and passions, the lower region of the inner man, while reason and conscience and volition are assigned to the spirit. Some suppose the soul and spirit united constitute the undying, imperishable part of man, while others maintain that the soul perishes with the body, and that the spirit only enters into a future life.

In our discussion of the question, we propose to turn from the conflicting opinions of uninspired men, and consult only the Divine Oracles. These contain, in our estimation, the most clear, definite, positive information on the subject, to be found anywhere. Our first inquiry is,

WHAT IS THE SOUL?

The soul is an organic essence, substantial but not material. The word soul (Hebrew, Nephesh; Greek, psuche) is applied, in the scriptures, to every creature that has animal life. In the fifth epoch of creation, God said (Gen. i., 20,) "Let the waters bring forth abundantly the moving creature that hath Nephesh, soul; and in the sixth epoch (Gen. i., 30), when the creation was completed, God gave the green herb for meat to every beast of the earth, every fowl of the air, and every thing that creepeth upon the earth, wherein there is Nephesh, soul. Every beast of the earth, every fowl of the air, and every thing that creepeth upon the earth, then, has soul. Does this include man? In Gen. ii., 7, we read, "And the Lord God formed man of the dust of the ground, and breathed into his nostrils the breath of life, and man became a living soul," (Nephesh). Since, then, brutes and men alike have souls, the inference is safe that some of the predicates of this word will be found in every creature that has animal life. This does not necessarily imply that all its predicates must be found in each living creature, since the diversity of capacity, in the different orders of the animal kingdom, is almost infinite. The soul of the snail can not be as comprehensive as the soul of man. It is, nevertheless, a soul; and, reasoning from analogy, some of the predicates of the soul of man should be found also in each brute.

What, now, are the facts in the case? Inquire carefully into the psychology of brutes and note what you find. The brute sees, hears, feels, tastes, smells, perceives, thinks, experiences pleasure and pain, joy and sorrow, delight and anger, desire and gratification of desire, arrives at conclusions which is a function of reason, plans and executes plans, makes choices and forms purposes; and all these in the exercise of mere constitutional endowments. Of course the scope and limit of these psychological manifestations are always determined by the endowment of each individual. Note now, the agent of all these activities in the brute is the soul. Not one of them can be predicated of the body.

Turning our attention to man, we find all

these activities predicated of his soul. The soul is the real man, the inner man, the seat of thought, the center of feeling, the throne of judgment, the mysterious subjective *Ego*, that wills, and originates all the choices and activities of the entire organism.

At this point I want to make a suggestion to psychologists. They uniformly use the word mind, instead of soul, to represent the thinking, feeling, willing man. From careful study of the scriptures, I believe this is an error. The scripture discrimination, when carefully studied in the languages in which they were written, is this:—The three activities—thought, emotion, volition—are attributed to the soul. The soul thinking is the mind. The soul in the exercise of emotion is the heart. The soul willing is the responsible man. The whole constitutes the moral agent. This distinction, it is true, will call for a different translation of several passages of scripture, a revision of definitions in our dictionaries, and some changes of phraseology in theological statements, as well as a new work on psychology, but what of that? Should not all these, and common parlance too, conform to truth, at whatever cost? This is surely the best, if not the only, way to let light in upon dark places. Ignorance and error are darkness; knowledge and truth are light. Let the light shine.

The soul, then, is the one mind psychologists tell us about, having three capacities, three modes of activity—thought, emotion, volition. All psychological exercises, active and passive, are attributed to it. In the soul lies the individuality; in the case of man, the personality. Man *is* soul; he *has* body and spirit. The admission of these facts, and they can not be successfully disputed, necessitates a conclusion that, used logically, must inevitably clear away the bewilderment and perplexity with which this question has for ages been invested, and establish, beyond dispute or doubt, the doctrine of the trichotomy of man.

Before passing to our next inquiry, it may be well to note that the word soul is often used to denote the whole man. "All the souls of the house of Jacob, which came into the land of Egypt, were three score and ten," (Gen. xlvi., 46:27), is only one of a large number of instances of this usage. Our next inquiry is

WHAT IS THE BODY?

The human body is a material organism, adapted to the uses of the human soul, in the present state or stage of its existence. It is the house in which the soul lives, its material dwelling place, while passing through its mortal life. Through the material organs of sense—the nerves of sight, hearing, tasting, smelling and feeling—the soul becomes conscious of the material universe, and acquaints itself with the qualities and attributes of matter, in its various forms, changes, uses and laws. These are its receptivities. By means of other organs of the body, each soul manifests to other souls the products of its own three modes of activity—intelligence, sensibility and will. These are its activities. By a mysterious and, up to this time, inexplicable connection, the soul imparts to the body a condition that we call life, rendering the body thoroughly subservient to the uses and will of the soul, within certain prescribed limits of activity. On this account the word soul is used to signify life itself, *anima*, as well as the living creature, *animus*. This life is declared in the scriptures to be in the blood. In Lev. xvii., 11, we read, "The life of the flesh is in the blood;" and in Deut. xii., 23, "The life is the blood."

Now, mark well, right here, though the soul gives life to the body, and uses the body as the servant of its own purposes, it imparts to the body none of its own powers or functions. The body knows nothing, feels nothing, wills nothing. The soul is a vital essence, the body a mere instrument. Subservient to the will of the indwelling soul, the body is as the staff in the hand, without knowledge, without feeling, without motive, without purpose, without accountability. The third and last constituent of man is

THE SPIRIT.

The Hebrew word translated spirit is Ruach, the Greek, pneuma. The thing thus named is, like the soul, an organic essence, substantial but not material. We come now to disputed ground; the real nature and offices of the human spirit. That much error exists here is evident from the fact that scarcely two writers on the subject agree. Of all the theories advanced, only one can be true, and our opinion is that not one of them all is true.

The spirit is the distinctive feature of man, the element of his constitution that makes him human. All the characteristic differences that distinguish men from brutes are effected through the spirit, due to it. These differences are not inherent in the spirit; but the presence of the spirit, as a distinct part of the man, furnishes the necessary occasion for the differences. It supplies the conditions that enable the soul to exercise those functions that do not belong to the brute, and that we call human. Respecting the spirit we note the following peculiarities:

1. It is a human spirit. It is not the spirit of God, nor in any sense the Divine spirit. It is not "a spark of divinity," struck off from the Divine mind, and implanted in man. In the scriptures, it is

never called the Spirit of God, nor a Divine spirit, but often the spirit of man. It pertains to and is found in no other creature than man. To him, however, that is, to his manhood, to everything that elevates him above the condition of a brute, everything that we call human, it is essential.

2. The spirit of man is the gift of God. In Zechariah xii., 1, we read, "The Lord formeth the spirit of man within him." In Numbers xvi., 22 and xxvii., 16, he is called "The God of the spirits of all flesh"; in Hebrews xii., 9, "The father of spirits"; and in Ecclesiastes xii., 7, we are told that, at death, "The spirit shall return to God who gave it." This is language that is never used with reference to the soul, and seems to intimate that, while the soul and the body are the product of generation, the spirit is given, as in the case of Adam, when God breathes into his nostrils the breath of life, and man becomes a living soul. As to the exact time when the spirit is given, is implanted in man, whether before or at the time of birth, we have no hint, and it would be folly to be wise above what is written.

3. The uses of the spirit are plainly indicated in such passages as these: Job xxxii., 8, "There is a spirit in man, and the inspiration of the Almighty giveth them understanding." Romans viii., 16, "The Spirit itself beareth witness with our spirit." A very significant and impressive text is Proverbs xx., 27, "The spirit of man is the candle of the Lord."

The idea that I get from these passages is that the spirit of man is the medium of communication between the spirit world and the soul of man, just as the body is the medium of communication between the soul and the material universe. This is the key to all that is new in my theory and treatment of this subject. The human spirit is not an intelligence. We have seen that all intellectual, emotional and volitional powers and functions are predicted of the soul. Can they, or any part of them, belong to the spirit also? It is too clearly a matter of course for argument, and almost too manifest to require statement, that no instance can be found, in all the handiwork of God, where he has duplicated his work by endowing with the same faculties or functions two distinct elemental parts of the same creature. If the soul thinks, the spirit does not think. If the soul feels, the spirit does not feel. If the soul wills, the spirit does not exercise the power of volition. The soul of the brute does all these things; and can the soul of man do less?

Moreover, since the soul is furnished with material organs, through which to hold communication with material existences, is not that very fact a hint that it must have spiritual organs through which to hold communication with spiritual existences? If such organs are necessary, where shall we look for them, but in the spirit? What other rational use can be found for the spirit? The perplexing question, in all ages, has been, What are the functions or uses of the spirit? and for lack of a rational and consistent answer to this inquiry the most absurd theories have been devised, we may with propriety say, "conjured up." The one fundamental error, lying at the bottom of all these theories, is the assumption that the spirit is endowed with intelligence; that it is a part of the mind, and that certain mental and moral attributes belong to it. Yield this point, abandon this hypothesis, and the whole subject is cleared of mist and doubt immediately.

4. We are now prepared for our last and most startling statement. It is this: The spirit of man is the spiritual body, spoken of by the Apostle Paul, 1 Cor. xv., 44, "There is a spiritual body." We support this proposition by the following considerations:

(1) The spirit, as already shown, is the medium of the same receptivities and the agent of the same activities, in the spiritual world, as the body is in the material world. Through the organs of the spirit the soul sees spiritual objects, hears spiritual voices, feels spiritual influences, tastes the heavenly manna that sustains the spiritual life, and smells the odors that are exhaled from the fields of Paradise. By means of the spirit it manifests to the spiritual world, and to this world also, its choices of good or evil, and its works of righteonsness or of iniquity.

The generally received idea is that the

spiritual body will be given to man at the resurrection and not before. Undoubtedly that is the body with which he shall come forth. The error lies in the hypothesis that he has no spiritual body now. The Apostle says, "There is a spiritual body," not, There shall be a spiritual body.

(2) That the functions of the human spirit are analogous to those of the human body is, also, a most convincing evidence that the human spirit is the spiritual body. Why should the organism through which the soul manifests itself be called a body in the one case and not in the other? Moreover, if there is a spiritual body, what can it be, and what must be its object and uses, other than such as are predicated of the spirit? and if the object and uses are the same, must not the substance be the same also?

THE MAN COMPLETE.

A complete man now stands before us, tripartite in his constitution, and with each of his three elemental parts distinctly defined. Whatever defects may be found in our theory, whatever it may lack of commending itself to the superior judgment of my fellow-seekers after truth, it certainly has this merit; the sphere and scope of each concept is clearly consistent and definite. Confusion of contents is impossible. This is strong evidence of its truth; and more than can be said in favor of any other theory that has ever been presented. Does error ever resemble truth so closely, in these respects and particulars?

Whether this is the true man—man as God made him—must, however, be further tested, by careful inquiry as to whether he is competent, in the relations and uses of his several parts, and under his circumstances as related to God and to his fellow-men, to meet the demands of his situation. If he fail in this particular, the failure must be admitted to be complete. It matters not how fine a piece of mechanism may be constructed, nor with what ingenuity and skill its parts may be adapted and adjusted, each to the others, if the machine fail to perform the work it was devised and intended to perform, it must be pronounced a failure. On the other hand, if it accomplish the purpose for which it was constructed, and surpass all other machines ever constructed for that purpose, its success should be frankly acknowledged, though the model should be quite new and unlike any that had preceded it. Have I not a right to demand the application of the same principle, in regard to this subject? If others dare submit their theories to this test, I will cheerfully take my chances. We proceed then, to inquire, Can this man be

A MORAL AGENT?

Here our triumph is complete. He not only can be, but he must be a moral agent: and the how and the why are so easily explained that a child can comprehend and understand the problem and its solution. The mysteries of self-consciousness, consciousness of right and wrong in self and others, reason, will in liberty, that is, in the presence of an alternative, conscience, accountability, sin, regeneration, holiness, and all the potentialities, experiences and activities, that distinguish man from the brute, and ally him to angels and to God himself, are made so plain, so easy of comprehension, that wayfaring men, though not blessed with high literary attainments or scholastic degrees, may revel in them with delight.

The brute is di-chotomous, constituted of soul and body only; hence desire and volition are prompted in one direction only. His intercourse is with the material world through the material body; hence no alternative is possible. Every desire has its origin in the flesh, is of the earth earthy; and the will, without opposition, assents to its gratification. Volition is possible only in this direction; and the whole life is necessarily sensuous. Desire is checked only by instinct; and volition, by experience. Painful consequences may lead to self-restraint; but experience is the only school in which he learns. For these reasons, a choice, respecting which right or wrong could be predicated, such choice as would give moral character as its product, is impossible. Hence the brute neither is nor can be a moral agent.

In man the case is different. Through the spiritual body, in the use of spiritual senses, the human soul is in communication with spiritual things; while, at the same time, through the material body, in the use of physical senses, it is in communication with the world of matter and all that pertains to it. One soul dwells in two bodies. Two worlds, two spheres of life, two classes of influences, directly opposite in their character, the one earthly and degrading, the other spiritual and ennobling, lie open before him, and urge their claims upon him. Thus he has an alternative. The conditions of actual choice are now fulfilled. The sovereign Will now asserts itself in liberty, under a solemn sense of responsibility. Reason weighs the consequences of either choice. Conscience presents its smiling approval, on the one hand, or its terrible scorpion sting, on the other. The enlightened soul is conscious that it is standing face to face with a terrible alternative, involving, as the consequences of its choice, the approving smile or the condemning frown of Almighty God.

This is Moral Agency, pure and simple, with all its necessary conditions. The soul, in the exercise of its sovereign functions, sits upon the throne of judgment; while the flesh, on the one hand, pleads for sensuous, degrading indulgence, and the spirit, on the other hand, moved by influences from above, pleads for righteousness, truth, purity, virtue. "The flesh lusteth against the spirit, and the spirit against the flesh, and these are contrary the one to the other." Thus situated, thus influenced, the soul makes its fearful decision, with character as the immediate and eternal destiny as the ultimate result. Such choice is possible only to a moral agent. Verily, this is the true man, God's man, fully competent for all the demands of his Creator.

CERTAIN PASSAGES OF SCRIPTURE.

Respecting certain passages of scripture, of which there is a very large number, that attribute intellectual processes, emotional experiences, and volitional functions to the spirit, they are to be disposed of in the same way as we dispose of the passages, of which there is also a large number, that attribute the same functions to the flesh. The ear hears, is attentive, seeketh knowledge, is obedient, understands, receives the word of the Lord. The eye sees, perceives, waiteth for the twilight, gave witness, is bountiful, mocketh, is satisfied or not satisfied, doth spare or not spare, mourns, offends. The mouth tastes, speaks wisdom, speaketh lies, is froward, is wholesome or perverse, is deceitful, unruly. The hands shed innocent blood, and the feet run to evil. Thus the various members of the body are accredited with nearly all the intellectual activities of the soul; yet, everybody knows that these organs are no more responsible for a single one of them than the bludgeon, in the hand of a highwayman, is responsible for the death of the unfortunate traveler who is smitten to the earth by it. Thus it is, also, with the spirit. It faints, revives, is troubled, is sad, is sorrowful, is joyful, is willing or rebellious, is hasty or patient, is haughty or humble, is steadfast or not steadfast, is faithful, excellent, dilligent, fervent, broken, contrite. Yet, all these, like those mentioned above, are the functions of the soul, not of the spirit.

This remarkable analogy, the use of the

same trope, metonomy, in both cases, to express acts, experiences and functions of the soul—in the one case as related to the material world, and in the other as related to the spiritual, is another evidence, of great force and weight, in support of our hypothesis that there is now a spiritual body, as well as a temporal or material, and that the soul lives in and uses either or both, in the alternatives of life, as occasions may afford opportunities; and that its experiences are according to its choices, influenced also by its environments.

If this is not the ideal man, as he came from the hand of his Creator, and was declared to be "very good," we challenge the world, especially those who refuse to accept our theory, to construct one, who shall more completely meet the demands of the situation, and for each particular of whose make-up a better reason can be found than we have given.

LECTURE III.

THE FALL.

The foreseen (not necessary) result (not consequence) of the creation of moral agents actually occurred. Man fell from his first estate. Using his power of freedom of choice, he chose to disobey his Creator, his King, his God. Respecting the nature of this transaction, great men, good men, have differed widely. It is a matter of sincere congratulation, to-day, as we believe, that those differences are gradually but rapidly disappearing. This is due largely, if not wholly, to a better understanding of the nature of moral agency than the world has ever had before. In this lecture we propose to examine, in the light thus shed upon them, the facts respecting this fall, as they are made known to us in the scriptures.

1. Our first inquiry will be respecting the moral condition of Adam and Eve, in the garden of Eden, as they came from the hand of their Creator, before they had exer-

cised a single choice, of which moral character could be predicated. They were furnished by their Creator, as we have seen (Lecture I.), with the endowments necessary to moral action; namely, intelligence and free will. They were surrounded by circumstances that furnished the necessary alternative of choice. The fair fruit of "the tree of the knowledge of good and evil" hung temptingly before their eyes. No alternative involving a moral choice had ever been presented before. No character had been formed. The wily serpent, endued with Satanic power to charm and deceive, declared to them, "Thou shalt not surely die." The moment of decision had arrived. The momentous choice to obey or disobey the command, "Thou shalt not eat thereof" awaits only the action of the will. What was their moral state, at that interesting moment?

The answer usually given to this inquiry is, "God created them holy." This is a great and fundamental error; and like every other error has been the source of incalculable mischief. God never created an intelligent being holy. From the very nature of holiness, as an attribute of a moral agent, that is an impossibility.

Holiness is a quality, or attribute, of character acquired by obedience. They were not holy for they had performed no act of obedience. Nor were they sinful, for they had, as yet, disobeyed no mandate. They were children, in development, that had just reached the moment, at which accountability commences. They were simply INNOCENT. (Why could not theologians have discovered that a thousand years ago? How much of error and confusion and strife it would have prevented).

Should the question arise, Was there, at this time, any natural inclination to either holiness or sin? the answer must be an unequivocal No. In their constitution there could be no bias; and heredity had not even commenced its work. It was just as natural, just as easy, for them to do right as wrong.

2. Our next inquiry is respecting the temptation; and our first postulate respecting it is, Temptation is impossible where there is no alternative. The necessity of an

alternative, in order to the development of moral character, has been clearly shown in Lecture I. The alternative, in this case, is furnished by the prohibitory command, Gen. iii. 16, 17, "Of every tree in the garden thou mayest freely eat; but of the tree of the knowledge of good and evil, thou shalt not eat of it; for in the day thou eatest thereof thou shalt surely die."

At this point in our inquiries, it should be stated that, while this transaction clearly illustrates the nature of an alternative, and is recorded in order to make that nature evident to all, we are not to suppose that no other form of alternative would have served the same purpose. From the temptation of our Saviour we may learn that at least three kinds of alternative may be employed, to test the loyalty of the soul to its God; namely, the appetites of the flesh, the ambitions of the soul, and presumption. It is evident, also, that these tests may be employed in almost innumerable forms. One form, however, is sufficient as such test; for he who disregards the mandate of his Sovereign in a single instance makes his lack of loyalty evident. Whether innocent or holy before, he is a sinner now.

3. The transgression. They disobeyed the command of their God. This was sin. "Sin is the transgression of law." 1 John iii. 4.

4. The consequences. With the very purpose to pluck and eat that forbidden fruit, innocence took its flight. As soon as the act was committed, a terrible consciousness of guilt, fearfulness, uneasiness, shame, horror, seized upon them. This was conscience. They had shown themselves unworthy of the confidence and approving smile of their best friend, their Creator, their God. What could now be done? The dreadful act could not be recalled. Despair, dark and dreadful, hovered over them as a cloud; surrounded, enveloped them as midnight. When they heard the sound of the approaching footsteps "of the Lord God, walking in the garden in the cool of the day, the man and his wife hid themselves from the presence of the Lord God amongst the trees of the garden." No one can imagine their feelings, at that moment, who has not

known, in the very depths of his soul, the awful meaning of the words "condemned already."

5. This loss of God's favor is called death. It was the execution of the predicted penalty, "In the day thou eatest thereof, thou shalt surely die." The propriety of giving this name, death, to the condition into which they brought themselves by the foolish and wicked act of disobedience they performed, will be apparent to any one who will give it a little careful, close thought. The Psalmist says (xxx. 5), "In his favor is life." If the favor of God is life, the loss of that favor must be death. This is the exact concept of these two words, wherever found in the scriptures, used in a spiritual sense. Life is the favor of God; eternal life is the favor of God extended through eternal ages. Death is the loss of that favor; eternal death is alienation from God perpetuated, by the continued, persistent choice of the rebellious spirit, through the ages of eternity.

Misled by an erroneous interpretation of Romans v. 12, "By one man sin entered into the world, and death by sin," many have supposed the death here predicted included temporal death, the death of the body; and that the mortality of the race is due to that transgression, and is a part of the penalty. Common, almost universal, as these opinions are, we must here record our dissent from them, and state our reasons for our dissent.

We firmly believe that Adam was just as mortal before he sinned as he was afterwards. Whether it was possible for him to protract his earthly life indefinitely, by eating of the fruit of "the tree of life," we will not stop now to discuss. Our reasons for believing that he was mortal are the following:

(1). This transgression did not bring physical death into the world. It is impossible to so interpret the language of the apostle, above quoted. The science of geology furnishes evidence, just as indisputable as the inspired word of God, that death had prevailed over animal life for unknown ages before the earth was in condition to be occupied as a residence for human beings. Eleven miles in thickness of the earth's crust was made of the remains of animals that died ages before God said, "Let us make man"; and they are to be found to-day incorporated into some of the great mountain ranges of the earth. This is a fact so well known that a single citation of evidence to support it is unnecessary.

(2). The body of Adam was made of the same "dust of the ground" as the bodies of the dead animals, whose remains, at that very time, he was treading beneath his feet; the same as that of which every mortal body, whether of brute or man, has been "formed" from the introduction of animal life into the world unto the present time. Why should the body of man, whether in innocence, holiness, or sin, be less perishable than that of the brute, which is made of the same material, the same chemical elements? It is the nature of everything that is formed of matter, and endowed with life, whether it be animal or vegetable, to grow until it reaches a state of maturity, then descend the scale of life, by regular degradations, until life becomes extinct, and "dust returns to the earth as it was."

Suppose that, in one of the great seismic upheavals of the earth's crust, that must have been very frequent at that period, the earth had opened beneath his feet, and Adam had been swallowed up in the chasm, and crushed to powder between the tumbling rocks, would it not have killed him? It is no answer to say that God would not have permitted such a catastrophy. To admit that the Providential arm was necessary to protect him is to admit his destructibility. Being the sovereign of his own choices, suppose he had determined to eat nothing, would he not have starved to death, just as you or I would? The supposition that he was not mortal is in itself an absurdity.

(3). The warning given them was, "In the day thou eatest thereof, thou shalt surely die." The meaning of many a prophecy has been clear only in its fulfilment. The only death that followed the transgression, "in the day" of its occurrence, was spiritual death, the loss of the favor of God. This may have hastened, undoubtedly did hasten, the dissolution of the body, but not to any great extent in the case of Adam, or of any of the antediluvians, of whom we have any record. Heredity had not done its fatal work at that time as it is doing it to-day.

(4). The reference to the literal rendering of the Hebrew, "dying thou shalt die," has no force whatever. The usage of that Hebrew idiom is solely that of emphasizing the fact expressed by the finite verb. It is correctly translated, "Thou shalt surely die"; and emphasizing the fact of dying must emphasize also the time of its occurrence. "To-day" does not mean any time within a thousand years. The death predicted came upon them at once. Commentators agree that its literal fulfilment was spiritual death, but usually assume that the seeds of decay and dissolution were at the same time sown in his body. This assumption is based upon the fact that he did die; a fact much more naturally accounted for on the ground that he was always mortal.

(5). Again, it is said that "Dust thou art, and unto dust shalt thou return," was a part of the penalty pronounced upon Adam for his transgression. From this interpretation I must also be permitted to dissent. Read the whole verse. Gen. iii. 19, "In the sweat of thy face shalt thou eat bread, till thou return unto the ground; for dust thou art, and unto dust shalt thou return." That little word "till" manifestly takes what follows it out from under the curse that precedes it, and refers it to the natural order of events that would have occurred, if no sin had been committed. That particular curse would rest upon him, until the close of his natural life. Then follows the statement, without any reference to the curse, given only as the reason why, in the nature of his constitution, he would and must "return unto the ground; for dust thou art, and unto dust shalt thou return." A careful study of Rom. v. 12-25, will also show that the more natural, if not the only consistent, interpretation of that whole passage is found on the hypothesis that spiritual death only is referred to. The death mentioned is the death that came "through sin; and so death, passed unto all men, for that all sinned." That spiritual death was the direct result of sin is not disputed; that physical death was, is contradicted by the very constitution of the human body. "Prove all things; hold fast that which is good."

LECTURE IV.

LAW.

This is God's world, God's universe. "The earth is the Lord's, and the fullness thereof; the world and they that dwell therein." He is sole proprietor and sole manager of the whole: the material and the immaterial; the animate and the inanimate; the intelligent and that which has no intelligence; the mortal and the immortal; the body, the soul and the spirit; the holy and the sinful; all are in his hands, subject to his government, creatures of his care. He is working the whole, managing the whole, with a definite aim and purpose, in the exercise of his own judgment as to what is best for each and for all; and with a freedom, independence, sovereignty, that is well illustrated by the farmer upon his farm, the mechanic in his shop, the merchant in his store, the teacher in the school-room, and the mother in the midst of her family and household affairs. Viewing God thus, seated upon his throne, at the head of the universe, the living, planning, guiding, controlling Manager, Director, Sovereign, of the whole, it is evident to the most casual observer and thinker that he must have many laws.

Of God's laws, there are three kinds, three distinct and separate systems: physical laws, ceremonial laws, and moral laws. These three systems of laws differ radically in their nature and object. We shall treat them separately, and in the order presented above.

I. Physical laws. These are (1) laws that seem to inhere in matter itself; and according to which the material universe is organized. As to their nature and practical utilities in human affairs, they are discussed at length and in particular in scientific works on Physics. The concept of physical law should include (2) every case where consequences necessarily follow antecedents, the relation being that of cause and effect. Our treatment of this class of laws will refer chiefly to their moral bearings. In this line of inquiry, it is important to notice the following:

1. Physical laws, whether considered as pertaining to events in the material, mental or spiritual world, are linked directly with the divine will, and are constant. Under similar circumstances or conditions, similar results may always be relied upon. Water, at a temperature of 32° Farenheit, with a downward tendency, will freeze; and ice, at the same temperature with an upward tendency, will melt. Mental inactivity will result in mental weakness. The wages of sin is death. These are examples of the constancy of physical law. They will always be true, whether in this world or any other.

2. The material universe is undoubtedly an immense system of object lessons; each law and each fact pertaining to matter corresponding with and intended to teach a fact or law pertaining to spiritual conditions and life. There is a very important sense in which Pope's view of the relations of God to the material universe is true, when he says,

"All are but parts of one stupendous whole,
Whose body Nature is, and God the soul."

With this view we conceive that a mote, a planet, a sun, a system of material worlds, each and all are as subservient to the will of God as my hand or my tongue is subservient to my will. Whatever may be the laws to which each mote or each world may be ordinarily subject, moved by the will of God it forgets them all, and leaps from its wonted course, as a railroad train leaps from its accustomed track when a sufficient obstruction lies in its way. He who made matter and the laws of matter is superior both to his work and to the laws that regulate it.

Nor is this power to work against "the laws of nature," as they are frequently called, found in God alone. We possess that power, and are continually using it. Thus, and thus only, do we employ the forces of Nature to supplement our own strength in any mechanical operation. While laws may be constant, the forces that may be brought to bear upon or against them are variable. These forces may or may not be sufficient to counteract and overcome the laws.

The force with which any portion of matter is attracted to the earth is called its weight. The force that may be exerted by a man in raising or attempting to raise a given portion of matter from the earth is called his strength. Now the strength of my arm may or may not be sufficient to raise one hundred pounds from the earth. If it is sufficient, I am able to overcome the law of attraction, as pertaining to that body. This shows that the laws of matter are not invincible. They may be overcome and rendered ineffectual; or they may be obstructed by an opposition not sufficient to overcome them, and their force employed to subserve the will of man, as when we use wind, water, steam, electricity, or the attraction of gravitation itself, to work machinery, propel vehicles of travel or transportation, convey messages, or for any other purpose.

These are the laws referred to, when people talk of the impossibility of God acting, except in accordance with his laws. As this is a very great and very damaging error, it is worth our while to give it some attention. Many, among whom may be found Christian people, and Christian ministers too, inquire in this wise: "How can such an event as men call 'special providence' occur? Will God disregard his own laws? Can I ask him to set aside a just penalty, that he has himself attached, as a natural consequence, to a righteous law, that I have broken? How can such a thing be? In this way God would undeify himself, abrogate his own statutes, destroy his own goverment. Prayer, in such cases, is not piety but presumption."

Now, what is the matter with people who talk thus? The error into which they have fallen may be a very natural one, but it is very mischievous. That error is the assumption that God is limited in his action by the laws here referred to—his physical laws. The remedy for this error is the fact stated above, that physical laws are not invincible. As regards the relation of a lawgiver to laws of his own enactment, bear this maxim always in mind, The law-giver is superior to his laws. Object lessons that teach this fact are abundant on all hands. They are found in every organized system of labor in the world. The farmer has laws for the management of his farm. The workmen in his employ are expected to conform their labor to these laws, unless excused from doing so, and he may generally observe them himself; but when the interests of the farm, the successful working of his plans, requires it, he disregards them utterly and gives new orders to his workmen. Thus he changes or disregards his own laws, according to the dictates of his judgment and the exigencies of occasions. The same is true of the mechanic, the merchant, the builder, the manager of a corporation, anybody who has workmen under him, and who says to one "Go, and he goeth, and to another, Come, and he cometh." This, in fact, is the meaning of the mysterious remark made by the Centurion to Jesus, Matt. viii. 8, 9. "Say the word, and my servant shall be healed. For I also am a man under authority, having under myself soldiers; and I say unto one, Go, and he goeth; and to another, Come, and he cometh; and to my servant, Do this, and he doeth it." What connection has this remark with his request that he should come and heal his servant?

His meaning is, The forces of Nature, the diseases with which men are afflicted, are subject to your will and word, just as servants who are under my authority are subject to my command. The forces of Nature are your servants, as these men are mine.

Perhaps the best illustrations of this principle and fact are found in the school-room and in the family. The teacher has many rules, and strictest observance of them is essential. Order is of first importance; and prompt, unquestioned obedience cannot be dispensed with. Still the teacher is superior to his law; and the fact is so fully recognized that no pupil hesitates, at any time when necessity or convenience requires, to ask release from obedience to any law; nor do the other pupils gape with wonder, when such request is granted. Precisely the same thing is true in the family. The numerous regulations that are necessary for the management of her multifarious and complicated household duties do not interfere with the ability of the mother to hear the petitions of her children, or of her servants, and perform acts of special providence for them, whenever the welfare of the family requires it.

All parental interests and functions belong to God, and what did Jesus say? "If ye know how to give good gifts unto your children, how much more shall your Father, who is in heaven, give good things to them that ask him?" The laws of Nature, as they are called, like the ordinary regulations of a family, are, under ordinary circumstances, adapted to and sufficient for the occasions that arise under them; but, when exigencies arise, and they prove inadequate, the higher interests of the souls of men call for the special providences of God. The law-giver is superior to his laws. Neither has God given to men powers that he does not possess himself. If men are superior to their laws, God is surely superior to his.

This view of the providence of God furnishest the only rational and consistent explanation of miracles. Instead of being "performed according to laws with which we are unacquainted," they are performed in accordance with no law at all. They are simply single instances, where God has performed an act, brought about an event, directly by the fiat of his Sovereign Will, regardless of, sometimes contrary to and in defiance of, his well established laws. The scriptures are full of examples that are thus, and only thus, to be accounted for.

What was the fiat, "Let there be light?" What was the flood? the building of the ark and the voluntary resort of the wild beasts of the earth to its sheltering apartments? What was the destruction of Sodom? the sparing and exaltation of Joseph and Moses? the burning bush? the giving of the law on Mt. Sinai? the manna in the wilderness? the healing by the brazen serpent? the heaping up of the waters of the Jordan? the tumbling down of the walls of Jerico? the fire from heaven that consumed the sacrifice of Elijah? the translation without death of Enoch and Elijah? the rescue of Daniel from the lions and of the faithful three from the seven-fold heated furnace? the delivery of Peter from prison and of Paul from the bite of the poisonous reptile? and the hundreds of other similar events that transpired in those days, and the thousands that have occurred since and are daily occurring in the experiences of God's people? what were they all? what are they now? but examples of the Will of God, meeting the necessity of a single case, by the exercise of his sovereign right, authority and power? THE LAW-MAKER IS SUPERIOR TO HIS LAWS. Nothing can can be more manifest to one who thinks, observes, and dares exercise the reasoning powers with which his Creator has endowed him than that every molecule of matter and every immense globe is just as obedient to the Will of God as my hand or my foot, when in a healthy condition, is to my will. Such is the relation of the Will of God to matter and to the laws of matter. Physical law is the immanent will of God. From all these facts it is evident that God is working out moral problems and not physical. The material universe was not made for itself. It has no value only as a means to moral ends. Hence it is that all its laws and interests yield, stand aside, when the higher demands and interests of moral, or sentient creatures of any grade require it. When we speak of "the good of being," only sentient beings are included. Inanimate matter, matter that is destitute of animal life, knows nothing of either good or bad.

2. Ceremonial laws. These may have their origin in the Will of God or the will of man. They may be enjoined by authoritative enactment or by common consent or custom. They may pertain to religious worship, social intercourse, courts of justice, and many other relations of human life. We shall consider them only so far as they may be the laws of God; that is, laws divinely enacted for the observance of his people.

Under the old dispensation, certain days were to be observed sacredly, in commemoration of important events; and certain sacrifices were required, some of them as grateful acknowledgements of divine blessings, others as typical of the great atoning sacrifice that was to be made in the fullness of time. Under the new dispensation, ceremonial laws, enacted by divine authority, are few. I find only the ordinances of baptism and the Lord's supper, unless marriage should also be included. All other requirements of the Christian religion come under the head of Moral laws.

The observance or non-observance of ceremonial laws may be ethical, not on account of the thing required, but because it is required. Our relations to God require that we respect his will, regardless of the thing he may have commanded. He has a reason for every command he has given; hence, when we cannot discover what that reason is, confidence iu his wisdom, and in his devotion to our welfare, as well as unquestioning loyalty to his Sovereignty, should prompt obedience; and neglect or refusal to recognize this obligation must be sin, however trivial the thing commanded may appear to us. When the Savior would wash his disciples' feet, Peter, undoubtedly feeling that the act, on the part of his Lord, was quite too menial, said, "Lord, thou shalt never wash my feet." The reply of Jesus was most remarkable, as indicating the fact that it matters not how trivial may be the act required, refusal to perform it is rebellion against the divine authority, and disloyalty to the government of God. "If I wash thee not," said he, "thou hast no part with me." This was a serious state of things, and Peter realized it. He did not wish to imperil the salvation of his soul for so trivial a matter as refusing to permit his Lord and Master to wash his feet; and with most humble submission he cried out, "Lord, not my feet only, but also my hands and my head." Thus a ceremonial law may also have indirect connection with moral character.

Ceremonial laws are symbolical. They employ a formal service to represent and impress spiritual ideas. Sometimes their purpose is the commemoration of an event that has already transpired; sometimes it is to symbolize an event, of which it is also prophetic; and sometimes both of these objects are included. The keeping of the passover illustrates the three ideas. It commemorates the sparing of the Israelites, when the destroying angle went through the land of Egypt, and slew the first-born of every family; it symbolized the salvation of believers and the destruction of unbelievers, under the gospel dispensation; and it was prophetic of the atonement that was to be made by the suffering and death of the "Lamb of God" on Calvary.

Ceremonial laws are also temporary. When the end is fulfilled for which they were intended, they cease to be obligatory. Christ fulfilled the ceremonial laws given to Moses, hence his followers never observe them. They are no longer obligatory. It is to this Jesus refers when he says, Matt. v. 17, "Think not that I came to destroy the law or the prophets: I came not to destroy but to fulfill.

3. Moral laws. The system of laws with which we have most to do, in the discussion of theological questions, is what are commonly called moral laws. This does not mean that these laws are moral or immoral; but that they are of such a nature that obedience to them cannot be refused without incurring guilt. When written, they define the duties that intelligent beings, moral agents, owe to one another, to themselves, and to the animal kingdom in general. This system of laws differs so widely from those

we have been considering, that very few, even of those "who seem to be pillars," have really apprehended their nature. They relate entirely to intelligent beings, who are able to comprehend the nature of a moral obligation. They are not the enactments of a Sovereign, nor are they established by the concurrent voice of a community, a nation, or the entire assemblage of all the intelligences in the universe. Yet they are uniform and universal. Wherever intelligent beings may be found, there these obligations exist. They are no respecter of persons. They are just as binding upon God and angels as upon men. They exist in the nature of things, have always been and will always be the same as they now are. They are immutable and eternal. No authority can abrogate them, no enactment set them aside. As they do not originate in a Sovereign Will, nor by any governmental authority, they are in no way or degree subject to any interference by any power in heaven or on earth.

Do you ask, Whence do they come? and how do they exist? I answer, they arise out of the relations of intelligent beings to one another. If there were but one sentient and intelligent being in the universe, there could be no moral law. If there were no sentient beings except brutes, there could be no moral law. Every obligation of man to God, of God to man, of man to man, or of man to brute, must arise directly and spontaneously out of the relations that each sustains to each and to all the rest; and perfect conformity, obedience, to these obligations, laws, on the part of those between whom the relations exist, is absolutely, immutably and eternally necessary to their happiness and welfare.

As the offspring of God, man owes allegiance, obedience, to him, as his Father, and his Sovereign Ruler. This is the prompting of love, as well as of a wise regard on the part of man, for his own happiness and well-being. These are the relations of man to God. The relations of God to man are those of a parent to a child, a King to his subjects who are dependent upon his providence for their existence and for the supply of every want of their natures. He is also related to them as the Infinite to the finite, the strong to the weak, the wise to the ignorant, the one in whose hands are all the resources of the universe to those who have no resources of any kind. These obligations rest upon him because he is a moral agent. A single instance of disregard or neglect of the welfare of one of his intelligent subjects would convict him of sin, and bring upon him self-condemnation and the condemnation of every intelligent creature in the universe. Hence we may well believe that "No good thing will he deny from them that walk uprightly." On the same principle, every sentient creature, even the most insignificant insect, is the object of his care; and "not a sparrow falls to the ground without his notice."

The relations of each man to each and all his fellows constitute the foundation of the obligations of each to all the rest. These obligations are found in the fact that the welfare of each of my fellows is as important to him and to all the rest as my welfare is to me and to all the rest. Every individual of our race is dependent upon the rest of the race, as well as upon God, for his or her highest well-being. Thus each is made to care for all and all to care for each. This is the moral law. Conformity to this law is the highest standard of human life, and promotes the most perfect condition of human welfare. This is the doctrine of both the first and second commandments, "Thou shalt love the Lord thy God with all thy heart, and thou shalt love thy neighbor as thyself." Thus "Love is the fulling of the law." It is also the doctrine of that wonderful paradox, the most extraordinary that ever fell from lips of clay, "He that seeketh to save his life shall lose it; and he that loseth his life for my sake shall find it." In the language of experience, as it appears in all the affairs of men, this may be paraphrased thus: Selfishness defeats the end at which it aims, but benevolence secures, without direct effort, the end at which selfishness aims in vain. It is found also in the language of the apostle, 1Cor. x. 33, "Not seeking mine own profit, but the profit of the many." This should be the aim, the purpose, the constant effort of every person of our race; and he who ignores this law, and refuses to accept it, and conform his whole life, in every wish, in every motive, in every act, to this obligation, stands convicted of sin, before his fellows, before his God, and before the bar of his own conscience. This is hell, as a condition of consciousness, whether in this life, or in the life to come.

Are these the laws of God? They are no more the laws of God than they are the laws of men and of angels. They grow spontaneously out of the relations of each intelligence to each and all the rest. No personal Sovereign has enacted them; and no power in the universe can either annul or change them. They are called the laws of God, because God, in fulfilment of the obligation resting upon him as Father, Sovereign, the Infinite, the All-wise, to seek and promote the highest happiness and well-being of his offspring, creatures, subjects, has promulged them, published them abroad, that we might know them, and be without excuse, if we disregard them. Apropos of this thought is the significant fact that the Hebrew word *torah*, translated law, signifies instruction.

God has ordained physical law by the immanence of his own sovereign will; he is also the author of certain ceremonial laws; but he has not enacted, nor even originated moral laws. These have their origin, even their suggestion, in relations. They grow from the intuitive affirmation of the reason of every moral agent in the universe, that rights may not with impunity, be violated by either God or angels or men. They may be called the laws of God only in recognition of the fact that he has made them known to us, and assured us that they must be regarded or evil consequences must follow:

This should be the understanding of monarchs and legislators. Their business as law-givers is not to make laws, except ceremonial laws. The only legislative authority with which they are invested, outside of ceremonial laws, is to ascertain what are the rights of their subjects, in their various relations to their sovereign and to each other, and require their observance. In the observance of these rights, each and all will find their highest well-being. Civil law is a branch of moral law.

The same is true in the family, the school, and wherever the authority of one person over another is recognized. Capital and labor may be perfectly harmonized on this principle, and no other. When this principle is fully understood and fully obeyed, by ruler and subject, by employer and employe, the millennium will be not a dream but a reality; and every recognition of this principle, and every effort to realize it, in the affairs of daily life, is a step in that direction.

This is also the key-note to a correct life, the key-note to a Christian life. It was sounded by Jesus when he said, "I came not to be ministered unto but to minister;" by Paul when he said, respecting Jesus, "He who was rich, for our sakes became poor, that we, through his poverty, might be rich;" and again by Paul when he said, "Ourselves your servants for Jesus' sake;" and again, "Not seeking mine own profit, but the profit of the many." This is the condition of things in heaven; and full and cheerful conformity to this principle will make any place in the universe heaven.

In the light of the above, we see how utterly unfounded and false is the assumption that the "Ten Commandments" were included in the law that was so fulfilled in Christ that it was no longer binding upon any body, Jew or Gentile. From the classification of laws, as given above, it is readily seen that such fulfilment could refer only to the ceremonial law. Neither of the other kinds of law could be included, because neither of them is capable of abrogation. Physical law must exist so long as effects follow causes; and moral law must be obligatory, in all its particulars, without any possible shadow of change, just so long as moral agents exist. In any particular relation it is the same, yesterday, to-day, and forever. The only question, then, as touching the decalogue, is whether it consists of ceremonial or moral precepts, whether they are edicts of ceremonial observances, or obligations that grow out of relations.

On examining the "commandments"

with reference to this point, no difference of opinion is likely to arise respecting any of them except the fourth. That there is something of the ceremonial in this, we freely admit. The seventh day was chosen as the particular day of the seven to be observed, "for in six days the Lord made heaven and earth, the sea, and all that in them is, and rested on the seventh day; wherefore the Lord blessed the Sabbath day, and hallowed it." This, however, was not the whole of it, nor the important part of it. If there had been no necessity for a Sabbath day, no day would have been named for its observance. The necessity of both labor and rest underlies the commandment, and that necessity is found in the relations of man to himself, his fellow man, and his God. Let us examine each of these points.

1. There is, perhaps, no physiological fact more clearly and firmly established than that the bodily welfare of a laborer demands that each seventh day be devoted to quiet and rest. Both mind and muscle, that are subjected habitually to severe taxation, day after day, must have one day in seven for

recuperation. We admit that it looks paradoxical, but experience has often proved its truth, that more work can be done in six days than in seven. Hence, rest on the seventh day is just as imperative, for one's welfare, as labor during the other six.

2. Consideration of the welfare of others, in every community, and of the world at large, imposes upon each member the obligation to observe the day of rest, and circumstantially the same day; because no one can disregard the precept without infringing upon the quiet, the repose, the rights of others. The moral law requires that the welfare of all (domestic animals included) must be regarded by each. On this point we find a very significant passage in Exodus xxiii. 12, "Six days thou shalt do thy work, and on the seventh day thou shalt rest, that thine ox and thine ass may rest, and the son of thy handmaid and the stranger may be refreshed."

3, The most sacred of all our obligations to "Remember the Sabbath day to keep it holy" is found in our relation to God himself. The idea is clearly expressed in Exodus xxxi. 13, 14, "Verily ye shall keep my Sabbaths, for it is a sign between me and you throughout your generation, that ye may know that I am the LORD that doth sanctify you. Ye shall keep the Sabbath therefore, for it is holy unto you." The history of the world shows that the human race "did not like to retain God in their knowledge." Knowing that this would be the disposition of men, God so constituted man that a periodical day of rest would be necessary for his welfare, and then gave him this commandment, that they might through its influence be helped to remember him, and keep the day sacredly, "keep it holy," as his day, not theirs. Hence he instructed them, Isaiah lviii. 13, "If thou turn away thy foot from the Sabbath, from doing thy pleasure on my holy day, and call the Sabbath a delight, and shalt honor it, not doing thine own ways nor finding thine own pleasure, nor speaking thine own words; then shalt thou delight thyself in the LORD, and I will make thee to ride upon the high places of the earth; for the mouth of the LORD hath spoken it."

For this reason, also, God has ordained

this day as a day of worship. Lev. xxvi. 2, " Ye shall keep my Sabbaths, and reverence my sanctuary;" xxiii. 3, " The seventh day is the Sabbath of rest, and holy convocation." Ezek. xlvi. 1, " The gate of the inner court that looketh toward the east shall be shut the six working days, but on the Sabbath it shall be opened." Thus rest and worship are required of men, not ceremonially, but for moral reasons; especially that men may remember their dependence upon God and their obligation, for their own physical and moral welfare, to reverence, adore, and love him.

The above discussion shows just where the falacy lies of those who contend so earnestly, and so conscientiously, that the Jewish Sabbath should still be observed. We have admitted that there is a ceremonial feature in the commandment. The day which the Jews were required to observe for rest and worship was the seventh day of the week, according to their reckoning, in commemoration of the day on which figuratively, God rested from the work of creation. While the command to observe a Sabbath is founded deep and solid on relations that make it a moral precept immutable, the day selected was a memorial day, subject to be changed or abrogated entirely. Hence, when the greater work of redemption was completed, and the ceremonial law nullified, the necessity of a Sabbath of rest and worship being the same as from the beginning, the most natural and appropriate thing imaginable was that the first day, as a memorial of the resurrection, should be appointed of God as the day on which such rest and worship should occur.

Apropos of this thought, let me here record a suggestion that has often impressed me deeply and solemnly respecting this change. No one is unaware of the deep-rooted prejudice that is formed by long-established habit, even when that habit is not sanctioned by divine authority. That such habit should be a thousand fold stronger, when sanctioned by divine authority, especially by direct and positive command, will also be admitted. The strength of the conviction, in every Jewish mind, that the seventh day, and no other, should be observed as the Sabbath, may be conceived in the light of these facts. Now lay beside these admissions the fact (undisputed, we think, by all who have not been deluded and deceived by the fallacies of modern sabbatarians) that from and after the resurrection, commencing on the evening of the very day on which it occurred, the followers of our crucified and risen Lord have observed the first day, as their accustomed day of rest and worship, with a unanimity that has never characterized any other similar change, in the history of the world. The efforts of late years to dispute this statement have resulted in masterly failures, for by far stronger evidence exists that for the first three hundred years after the ascension, no discension among the Christians of those early times had arisen on this question, while the evidences of its observance, during nearly all that time, are overwhelming.

My suggestion, based upon these facts, is, that this change was not without authority, as it is supposed to be. Every person is familiar with the fact that but a small portion of what our Savior said and did, while here upon the earth, was ever recorded. Paul exhorts the Ephesians, Acts xx. 35, "Remember the words of the Lord Jesus, how he himself said, It is more blessed to give than to receive;" a precept not found in either of the gospels. From the record given, we would naturally suppose that he was somewhere here on earth forty days after his resurrection, but of his words and works during that time we have almost nothing. Now, taking into consideration the fact that those Jewish followers of his, steeped in the habit that was originally instituted by God himself, and had come down to them through fifteen centuries, increasing in intensity all the way, of observing the seventh day as the Sabbath; is it supposable that they all, numbering five thousand within two months of his resurrection, prompted by no other idea than the propriety of commemorating the resurretion by that means, should agree, without dissent, to no longer keep the time-honored, heaven-ordained Sabbath holy, but transfer its honors and sacredness to the first day? and all this without a hint from their revered and mourned Lord and Master? Did not Jesus himself, in one, perhaps several, of the numerous interviews he must have had with his disciples, during those memorable forty days, suggest to them the propriety of such a change, substantiating the suggestion by showing them the greater importance of his resurrection over the creation rest day? Truly, I cannot conceive that so great, so important a change, could have been made, with such unanimity, upon any other hypothesis. Leaving out this suggestion, or rather instruction, from Jesus himself, and the effect is overwhelmingly too large for the the cause. The change could not have been made, so suddenly, so completely, so harmoniously, without his authority.

In concluding this Lecture, let me say, I hope those of my readers, who have doubted the divine authority and sanctity of the Christian Sabbath, because a direct command to keep it holy is not found in the New Testament, will consider the moral basis on which we have placed it. The relations of man to man, and of man to his God, were not affected in the least by the fulfilment and abrogation of the ceremonial law, the "law of commandments contained in ordinances." That which is ceremonial may pass away or be changed; but moral obligations are unchangeable and eternal.

LECTURE V.

PENALTIES.

Many erroneous notions prevail respecting the penalties that are attached to law, as the consequence of its transgression. The prevailing idea is that the infliction is intended to be of the nature of something deserved. "I will pay you for that," says one school boy to another, who has played some trick upon him. "There, take that," says a passionate parent to an unruly child; "it is not half what you deserve." A thief "deserves" imprisonment; a murderer "deserves" death. "Justice demands that law shall be satisfied." Now, we apprehend that all this is quite foreign from the divine idea of the consequences of transgression. Governments, including the divine government, exist for the welfare of the governed, not to gratify the ambition, sustain the dignity, or promote the glory of a ruler; nor to furnish occasion to wreak vengeance upon an offender. "Whosoever of you will be

the chiefest, shall be the servant of all."
One of the concomitants of the maxim,
"Might makes right" was "The chief end
of man is to glorify God." Undoubtedly
man should glorify his Creator, by devoting
himself to the end for which he was created,
but not by recognizing in him an arbitrary,
tyrannical Sovereign, who can be glorified by
the abject, slavish servitude of his subjects.
We think it is safe to say that, in all
the penalties attached to divine law, there
is no such principle recognized, or even
hinted, as punitive justice—the infliction of
pain, damage, discomfort or inconvenience,
simply as a punishment deserved—so much
pain for so much sin. All God's penalties
are corrective. First they warn the offender, chastening him for his profit. If he will
not be profited by chastisement, they cut
him down, as a warning to others, the welfare of the whole, the greatest good of the
greatest number, or the greatest profit to
the highest interests, being always the ultimate motive.

Penal, vengeful punishment, is inconsistent with and antagonistic to the nature of moral agency. Such punishment could have no other object, nor could it have any other effect, than to coerce the will, and compel an outward show of conformity to a requirement, through dread of consequences, while true obedience, obedience that can justly claim the reward of virtue, must be through love, engendered by a conviction of the judgment and a holy purpose of heart, conditions that can never be secured by the dread of punishment.

The divine idea of punishment, as stated above, is disciplinary; nothing more; nothing less. "It is for chastening that ye endure; God dealeth with you as with sons. . . . We had the fathers of our flesh to chasten us, and we gave them reverence; shall we not much rather be in subjection to the Father of spirits, and live? For they verily for a few days chastened us as seemed good to them; but he for our profit, that we may be partakers of his holiness" (Heb. xii. 7–10).

If asked how this view of God's dealings with transgressors, and especially with the incorrigible who will not be reformed, can be reconciled with passages that speak of God as "taking vengeance on them that know not God," as saying "vengeance is mine, I will repay," and many other like passages, I reply, just as we reconcile the very numerous passages that speak of him as "being angry," "the wrath of God," etc., with the fact that God is love, and is never moved by such passions as men call wrath and anger. Men seem often to forget that God loves the innocent as well as the guilty, the obedient as well as the disobedient, the loyal as well as the disloyal. "God is love;" "his tender mercies are over all his works." To protect the rights of the loyal, it is often necessary to so deal with the disloyal that they may be hindered from doing the harm they would be glad to do. "Surely the wrath of man shall praise thee; the remainder of wrath shalt thou restrain." So long as the wickedness of the wicked may be made to react upon the world for good, God permits the sinner to have his liberty and work his diabolical plots; but when that limit is reached, through love for the faithful, the welfare of the whole, he removes the worker of iniquity, and places him where his influence for evil will be restrained; at least, where it will not vex the righteous. This seems to short sighted mortals as wrath, anger, vengeance, and thus they have named it. The necessity of dealing thus with criminals is neither unjust nor strange nor mysterious.

There is not a government upon earth, that has not the same provision for dealing with the same class of characters. Who ever heard of a government, a state, a kingdom, that had not a prison, a place in which to confine incorrigible transgressors? Who denounces such a governmental arrangement as despotic, cruel, tyrannical? Hell is God's state prison. Some one has called it, with a propriety that all ought to understand and approve, "God's asylum for incurables." Nor is it necessary to drive, with force of arms, the finally impenitent into the dreadful pit of woe. As "like loves like," and "birds of a feather flock together," so each of them will "go to his own place" of his own accord, when he is no longer permitted to work his diabolical schemes for the ruin and destruction of others. Enter heaven? You could not force him through the pearly gates, to look for a single moment upon the glories of the saved, and listen to the praises of him that hath redeemed them.

People who can not endure the imperfect devotions of a prayer meeting, or the tedious story of the cross for an hour on a Sabbath morning, are not in much danger of being driven, except by their own inclinations, "from the presence of the Lord and the glory of his power." Heaven would be to them the severest part of hell. It is the compassion of God, even for those that hate him, and revile him, and curse him, that permits them to retire from the glory of his presence, which is far too bright for their diseased eyes, and take what comfort they can in the hateful society of one another. "He that sinneth against God wrongeth his own soul." With Judas they "go to their own place."

The object, therefore, of the penalties that are attached to God's laws, is (1) to prevent their transgression by fear of the consequences; (2) to cause the offender to relent and forsake his evil ways; and (3) to protect the innocent and loyal from the baleful and ruinous influences of the incorrigibly evil-disposed.

It should also be kept in mind that, while the means necessary for the protection and welfare of the loyal may not be regarded as the natural and necessary effect of sin upon the sinner, as "the wages of sin is death," neither are they to be attributed to anger, wrath, resentment, vengeance, and payment of deserts. No act of God, no treatment of either the righteous or the wicked, ever was or ever will be inconsistent with Infinite Love. The highest well-being, the greatest happiness, of the whole, and of each, so far as each will permit, is the ultimate motive and object of every thought, desire and purpose, of the Infinite Father and Sovereign of all.

LECTURE VI.

THE ATONEMENT.

We are now prepared for the discussion of what is justly regarded as the most difficult of all theological questions. Since God was fully aware, before he created man, that he would sin; and since the race was created for the happiness that would result from its existence, it is but natural to suppose that God would devise some way to counteract the effect of the fall, and even to turn this manifest evil to some good account. This is just what he did. The plan of redemption was not an afterthought. Without this the acme of his glory would not have been reached.

The problem of creation was a great one, but the problem of redemption was almost infinitely greater. This problem is the highest, the most sublime, the most difficult, of all the problems ever brought to the attention of a finite intelligence. Men think some of the questions presented for our solution in the physical and mental sciences great and difficult; but those found in the science of morals, especially those connected with the plan of redemption, are far more profound, and far more difficult of solution, or even of human comprehension, when revealed to us by him who alone was capable of solving it. "Concerning whose salvation the prophets sought and searched dilligently." "Which things angels desire to look into." The key to this whole plan of salvation is found in what is called the Atonement.

The word atonement had its origin in the Latin words *ad* and *unus*, from which our words *at one* were derived; and the syllables of the word — at-one-ment — express its exact meaning. The Greek word, *katallage*, also corresponds precisely to this signification. Our word reconciliation is its exact synonym. The idea contained in the word atonement, then, is that of the reconciliation of two parties that are at variance with each other. In order to understand the necessity and nature of this reconciliation, we notice,

1. The parties to be reconciled are God and man. The relations of these parties have been thoroughly discussed in Lecture IV.; and the manner of the alienation between them, in Lecture III. What we want now to emphasize is, "God is our Father and our Mother too." All the interests that parents feel in their offspring are properly predicated of him. These are all included in the word Love. This all-embracing word means, in this connection, supreme devotion to the welfare of his offspring, and divine sympathy with them in all their trials and sufferings. This interest in and sympathy for the human race is not in the least abated by the fact that "knowing God, they glorified him not as God, neither gave thanks; but became vain in their reasonings, and their senseless heart was darkened."

2. God's laws (We call them God's laws, not because they originated either in his will or in his love; (see Lecture IV.), but because he, speaking after the manner of men, discovered and revealed them to us), are all beneficent, adapted to our constitution and circumstances, and binding upon us both for

our own individual good and for the good of all intelligent beings, the Deity himself included.

3. In the exercise of their moral agency, men, individually, have disregarded, transgressed, these laws, and thus plunged themselves into misery, made others miserable, and entailed misery upon their posterity. This we call sin. In doing this each one for himself has lost the favor of God, incurred the disapproval of others, filled his own soul with all the horrors of condemnation, and bound himself with a chain that he is unable to sever. This is hell; and in this lost, helpless, hopeless state he must remain eternally, unless delivered by a superhuman, superangelic, super-finite, agency.

4. Notwithstanding his gauling, hateful bondage, his moral agency is not destroyed, not even impaired. Responsibility both for contracting his bondage and for remaining in it, still remains. Although he is absolutely unable to deliver himself from his deplorable condition, he can refuse to be reconciled to it, can strive against even the "sins that so easily beset him," and is in no

way curtailed in his ability to avail himself of any assistance that may be offered him. This condition is vividly described in Rom. vii. 14–16, 21–25. "We know that the law is spiritual; but I am carnal, sold under sin. For that which I do I know not: for not what I would, that do I practice; but what I hate, that I do. But if what I would not, that I do, I consent unto the law that it is good. . I find then the law, that, to me who would do good, evil is present. For I delight in the law of God after the inward man; but I see a different law in my members, warring against the law of my mind, and bringing me into captivity under the law of sin which is in my members. O wretched man that I am! Who shall deliver me out of the body of this death? . . . So then I myself, with the mind, indeed, serve the law of God, but with the flesh the law of sin."

This passage was, and that not far into the long ago, generally supposed to describe the prevailing Christian experience; and Christians who were "living in the 7th chapter of Romans," used often to quote,

"When I would do good, evil is present with me." They used, also, to sing with the humane and excellent Cowper,

> "'Tis a point I long to know,
> Oft it causes anxious thought,
> Do I love the Lord or no,
> Am I his, or am I not?"

and with Watts,

> "Dear Lord, and shall we ever live
> At this poor, dying rate?"

Doubtless many who "indulge a hope," whose names are found on rolls of church members, are still waging their warfare against sin, and the bondage of sin, from this disadvantageous front line of battle. The passage is intended, however, to describe the experience of a soul that is conscious of its bondage, and its own inability to escape therefrom; struggling for deliverance, and looking for assistance from some higher source. "Who shall deliver me out of the body of this death?" Death, moral death, is as a body, in which the soul is imprisoned, and from which it cannot be delivered, except by divine aid.

Perhaps we should call to mind, as we pass, that there are those who do not realize their bondage, and have no desire to be delivered from it. They have become infatuated with sin, are soured against holiness and everything that savors of holiness; "call evil good, and good evil; put darkness for light, and light for darkness." These have come into this state of moral depravity by their own voluntary choices. In the exercise of their moral agency they brought themselves into their delusions; and by the same means they remain there. Their freedom, as moral agents, is in no way destroyed or impaired by the blindness of their minds or the darkness of their understanding. Help is within their reach; they may avail themselves of it if they will; and they will be held responsible for their own ruin and despair, if they do not. If they persist in their delusion and willful stubborness, they are lost. They hate God and everything that God loves. Nothing can move them. They are incorrigible, incurable. Such are lost. There is no help for them; because they despise the "only name under heaven, that is given among men, wherein we must be saved." This rebellion against God and against all that is good is hell, whether in this life or any other, past, present or future; and since they are deathless in their very nature and constitution, their hell is, unavoidably and indisputably, eternal. They are fixed, unalterably and forever, in their purpose to have nothing to do with offers of pardon on condition of repentance. No atonement, no means of reconciliation, can reach them, or have any influence upon them for good. A truthful but terrible description of them may be found in the second chapter of the second epistle of Peter.

5. Just at this juncture, when the bound and fettered and helpless and lost soul is groaning and struggling for deliverance, Christ, "mighty to save," appears upon the scene. He comes to offer the necessary help. "Thou shalt call his name Jesus, it is he who shall save his people from their sins."

6. We are now ready to inquire what God wishes and purposes to effect through the gift of his Son as a "sacrifice for sin?"

(1) He does not wish nor purpose to do anything that will militate against the authority or dignity of his moral government, nor compromise justice, nor encourage sin, nor even the hope of escaping the penalty of sin, in such a sense that men shall be so much as tempted to "sin because grace abounds." None of these things can be done. To permit them, and especially to devise a plan by which souls might be saved at such an expense would make God himself the chief of sinners, a rebel against his own throne, and not against his own throne only but against the rights and welfare of every moral agent in the universe. The end and object of moral government must not be compromised.

Justice and Mercy are not at war with each other. There is no antagonism between them, in any sense or degree. They belong not only to God, to judges, to governments, and to all governmental officials, but to every intelligence in the universe; and if they were at variance, every intelligence, from God to the weakest, would be at war with himself. They are attributes of the same mind, and must work in harmony with each other. Mercy can never be shown until Justice is satisfied; nor Justice be executed until Mercy consents. So long as the objective ends of law and penalty can be gained by merciful means, retributive or punitive measures cannot be resorted to. To inflict death, suffering, disgrace, even annoyance or discomfort, upon an offender, when Justice might be satisfied without such infliction, would be itself injustice.

(2) It is his purpose to secure by merciful measures all that the most rigid execution of the natural penalties of law could effect, in the way of honoring the Sovereign, maintaining the dignity of the government, securing the welfare of its subjects, and at the same time make a loyal subject of the offender, thus compelling Justice to demand his release from the sentence that he himself had pronounced against him.

Let us illustrate this point by a supposed case in any human government. We have shown, in Lecture V., that the object of punishment is first to reform the offender, and secondly, in case the offender will not be reformed, but becomes dangerous to the welfare of community, to separate him from loyal and peaceable citizens, a state prison being provided for that purpose; thus securing peace, order and safety to good citizens, and doing a substantial favor to the offender himself. The motive to this apparently harsh procedure is in no sense, in no degree, malevolent. It is benevolent in every particular. The state does not exult, the citizens do not rejoice, in the sufferings of the culprit, however fiendish and incorrigible he may have shown himself, in fact they pity the poor, deluded victim of his own folly and depravity, and consent to his suffering only because that is the only way to assure themselves against his depredations. These are the ends that Justice demands, in any government, human or divine. Moreover, when these ends are secured, Justice is satisfied, and the end of this function of government, viz., the securing of the peace and welfare of its subjects, is fully realized.

Now, let us suppose that some Salvation Army General, or Captain, or private, should go to the prison, where these "poor sinners" against the peace and dignity of the state are shut in, that they may thus be shut out from the community whose welfare they refused to regard, and effect such a thorough reformation of the culprits there incarcerated, that each one should become a good, useful, industrious citizen, loyal to the state, true, noble, trustworthy, in every trait of his character. Would you, would anybody, object to the release of those prisoners? In their reformation is not every end of Justice effected more satisfactorily to the government, and to the community, than their lifelong punishment could effect it? How this illustration applies to the salvation of sinners against the government of God, and the welfare of men, thus explaining the philosophy of the atonement, we shall see as we proceed.

7. We are now prepared to note critically the exact situation.

(1) The sinner stands before the bar of God, "condemned already."

(2) Justice does not say, as has often been represented, "Cut him down." Instead of this, he turns to Mercy, with the anxious

inquiry "Can you do anything for him?" Mercy replies, "I will try."

(3) The Judge states the case. "This culprit has voluntarily, willfully, knowingly, inexcusably transgressed a righteous law, approved by every intelligence, good and bad, in the universe. He is not only convicted by unimpeachable testimony, but he frankly and honestly confesses his guilt. The penalty of this transgression, the justice of which is not questioned by any intelligence in the universe, is death. 'The wages of sin is death.' 'The soul that sinneth, it shall die.' This soul is imperishable in its nature. It is immortal. Its conscious existence can never have an end. He not only stands condemned before this high court, but every intelligent moral agent in the universe condemns him. In the depth of his soul he also condemns himself, and acknowledges the justice of the penalty (Rom. vii. 16). How forlorn, how desperate, how hopeless his condition. Unless he can be brought to repentance, he will only become continually worse and worse, until he shall join the company of those 'wander-

ing stars, for whom the blackness of darkness hath been reserved forever.' Mercy do thy best. If any way can be found by which I may be just and yet justify this poor, wretched, lost soul, find it."

(4) Justice addressing Mercy, "One thing, loving sister, you must bear in mind: I can consent to no terms, for the release of this culprit from his just deserts—eternal despair, that will, in any way or degree, militate against the rights or welfare of our Sovereign, or of the most insignificant subject of his kingdom, or of any soul in the universe, though it be in fiercest rebellion against him."

(5) Mercy responds: "Nor will I consent that he shall be delivered over to hopeless and eternal perdition, until every means that Infinite Love can prompt and Infinite Wisdom devise, for his restoration to loyalty and full reconciliation to thy demands have been exhausted upon him in vain."

8. When these demands of both Justice and Mercy are fully satisfied, nothing more is necessary, from whatever standpoint the transaction is regarded. If the sinner,

every sinner in the world, accepts the kind offices of Mercy and is saved, reformed in heart and life, changed to a good, loyal subject, Justice has no further demand upon him. That is itself the highest exhibition, the very end, of justice. The dignity of the government is not compromised; the wisdom of the Sovereign, in giving the law and proclaiming the penalty, is vindicated; transgression is discouraged; penitence encouraged, and every ideal of a perfect and righteous government, fully realized; the highest ideal of a perfect government being the greatest good of all concerned, Sovereign and subjects.

If, on the other hand, the offender spurns these gracious offices, every hope of Mercy is extinguished Everything has been done for the saving of the lost soul that Infinite Love and Infinite Wisdom combined could effect. The soul is lost by its own mad choice. "Madness is in their heart while they live; and after that they go to the dead."

9. The execution of this difficult task was committed to the second person in the

Godhead (See Lecture X.)—the Word of Creation, the Jehovah of Providence, the Christ of redemption — known when he "dwelt among us" as the Son of God and the Son of man. His human name was Jesus: "Thou shalt call his name Jesus, for it is he that shall save his people from their sins." Our inquiry now is, How did he accomplish this great work? What did he do, the result of which should be to save fallen men and women from sin and death?

(1) He assumed the form of man; dwelt on earth in a human body; was subject to all the desires, necessities and inconveniences of a human life; which to him must have been a humiliation, a self-denial, incomprehensible to us, and incomparable to any similar act of any other intelligent being of whom we have any knowledge.

Thus he came to us; became one of us; laid his hand upon us; bridged the chasm between divinity and humanity; manifested to our human senses the goodness, the wisdom, the love, the power to save, of the Infinite Father. By this mission the world, even in its rebellion and alienation, has been made acquainted with God, been made to understand what kind of a being God is towards us. The adage says, "There are those whom we do not like, because we do not know them, and we will not become acquainted with them, because we do not like them." Thus to the unregenerate soul, out of Christ, "God is a consuming fire;" but in Christ, as revealed to us through Christ, he is to us individually a loving Father. Jesus, the "mediator between God and men" (not man as a race, but men as individuals), has made us acquainted with him. With his divine right arm around the Father, he throws his human arm around the sinner, and brings the alienated parties together. This is atonement literally, in its true and highest sense; "according to the glorious gospel of the blessed God."

(2) His was a perfect life. "Tempted in all points, like as we are, yet without sin," he has shown us how to meet temptations of the devil, how to conquer the appetites of the flesh, how to rise above the degrading influences of the world, also how to sympathize with those who are in

distress, how to minister to those who are in want, how to deny ourselves for the good of others, how to lay down our lives if need be to save them, and how to trust him that life, thus sacrificed, will be restored to us again through a triumphant resurrection.

(3) The effect of this revelation of the true attitude of the Father; namely, that of love, love only and forever; towards deluded, fallen, wandering, lost souls; emphasized by the voluntary humiliation, cheerful self-sacrifice, patient suffering, exemplary life, wonderful doctrines, triumphant death and glorious resurrection, of his beloved Son, which constitute the influential means that Mercy employs, is more potent than all other influences, known or imaginable, to return wandering prodigals to their Father's house, induce reformation of character and life, save the world from rebellion, give stability to the government, and reflect highest honor upon the Sovereign, thus realizing every end and demand of Justice, and at the same time securing the atonement, reconciliation, of disloyal, rebellious souls to their God, Father, Sovereign, by changing them, con-

verting them, into loyal, loving, obedient subjects of his kingdom. Is not such a work of redemption, whereby it is so clear, and so easily comprehended too, that "he might be just, and the justifier of him that believeth in Jesus," the most sublime of all his work, the crowning glory of our most glorious Sovereign, God and Father?

10. To make this theory of the atonement clearer to all, and establish its truth more firmly in the minds of all, as well as to remove some objections, let us consider the following facts and circumstances:

(1) While the offer of atonement, the conditions of reconciliation, are made available by every sinful son and daughter of Adam, they elect, individually, whether they will avail themselves of the offer, and comply with the conditions or not. Hence, the demands of Justice are met, through the working of these merciful agencies, only in the case of those who accept them. The natural consequences of persistent disloyalty cannot be averted. The just condemnation of the incorrigible is made doubly reasonable by the fact that they sinned

willfully at the first, and willfully and stubbornly refused to accept Mercy's offer of pardon and reconciliation, thus adding greatly to their guilt.

In their case, Mercy retires weeping from the scene, and sorrowfully consents that the sword of Justice must be allowed to do its fatal work. "These shall go away into eternal punishment" (Mat. xxv. 46). This is all the satisfaction Justice has in their case. How unsatisfying it must be, as compared with that which is experienced in the case of those that are saved. Justice himself weeps as he executes the dreadful penalty. For we must still bear in mind that Justice, as truly as Mercy, is an attribute of Love. "I have no pleasure, saith the Lord, in the death of him that dieth." God's love for both the loyal and rebellious requires that the latter be placed in his state prison, his Asylum for the incurable, where they can do no harm.

(2) It is well known that Love, when appreciated, is vastly more potent to secure obedience, that is, to prevent disobedience, than threats of the severest punishments that

could be inflicted. Call to mind also, in passing, that the obedience of love is obedience, that of fear, even when perfect in form, is not ethical obedience, because it lacks the spirit of obedience. In the gift of his Son, to bring his offer of a merciful salvation to a lost world, God has made such an exhibition of regard for the welfare and happiness of our fallen race as no mind, except the Infinite, could ever have thought of; and to which nothing but Infinite Love could prompt. Moreover, the love of the Father is still further intensified and emphasized by the Son, in the cheerfulness with which "he who was rich for our sakes became poor, that we, through his poverty, might be rich;" "who, existing in the form of God, counted not the being on an equality with God a thing to be grasped, but emptied himself, taking the form of a servant, being made in the likeness of men; and being found in fashion as a man, he humbled himself, becoming obedient even unto death, yea, the death of the cross." "I lay down my life, that I may take it again. No one taketh it away from me, but I lay it down of myself." "He offered up himself."

What wonder that such a manifestation of such love should challenge the admiration of all the intelligences in the universe! What wonder that "we love him, because he first loved us!" Thus the reason becomes evident why the atonement is more potent to prevent sin than the execution of the penalty of the law. It is a fact well established in the experience of every moral agent that a willing, grateful, loving devotion to a parent or a teacher renders its possessor more attentive to opportunities to show that devotion by acts of loving obedience than the strongest influence of a threatened punishment can be to put one on his guard against temptation to disobedience. The contrast between these two states of mind and their influence to prevent transgression is marked and significant. The one is a fixed, living, ever active desire for an opportunity to please the law-giver; ever on the alert, with "Here am I send me" glowing in his heart and shining in his anxious eyes and countenance; the other is longing for the forbidden fruit, and hating both the law and the law-giver that prohibit it. In this attitude, what wonder that "when temptations come in like a flood," when lusts burn for indulgence, when resentment of wrong or insult, actual or fancied, suddenly bursts forth into an uncontrollable flame of anger, a reckless spirit gains full possession and all the dire consequences of disobedience are, for the moment, forgotten.

(3) It is also a fact that the soul that is moved by grateful love to loyalty resents with firmest purpose influences to disloyalty. Such a soul is not "empty, swept and garnished;" it is full. Every recess is occupied with hearty, loving, irresistible, ever active devotion to loyal obedience. Its language is, "What shall I render to my God for all his benefits?" a state of mind that is more reliable and efficient to secure obedience than the strongest resolution possible, to escape a penalty, while burning with desire for the forbidden object.

(4) Another fact of great significance and power is that rescue from danger, the saving of one's life, is the most potent of all

things to beget and perpetuate in the heart of the saved, that loving devotion to the Savior, that secures the most perfect service possible.

(5) The accumulated influence and power of all these facts are an ample substitute, in the practical working of the atonement, for the severest penalty of the most aggravated offence. Who can, for a single moment, doubt the superiority of this substitute over the execution of the penalty, to prevent transgression? This being the case, Justice is not only satisfied, but rejoices to accept it. A better end is reached than Justice ever dreamed of in this particular. This is Mercy's triumph No. 1.

(6) The atonement vindicates the righteousness of the law and the wisdom of the penalty attached to it. In the light of these persistent efforts to save the sinner, efforts to which the offended Sovereign was moved by motives which the selfish heart, while in its willful and wayward course of selfish indulgence and haughty defiance, could neither consider nor appreciate; and still further impressed by the gratitude and

blessedness of the saved, even the lost are compelled to acknowledge the complete satisfaction of Justice, as shown in the case of the saved, and the wisdom of both the law and the penalty, as visited upon themselves. While those who "stand upon the sea of glass, having the harps of God, sing the song of Moses, the servant of God, and the song of the Lamb, saying, Great and marvelous are thy works, O Lord God, the Almighty; righteous and true are thy ways, thou king of the ages," not a word of complaint of injustice comes from those who are hieing away "from the face of him that sitteth on the throne, and from the wrath of the Lamb." Every intelligence in the universe, that has any knowledge of the transaction, acquiesces in the final decisions of "that great day." This is Mercy's triumph No. 2.

(7) The plan of salvation, through these merciful agencies, moves the sinner to penitence; and "godly sorrow worketh repentance unto salvation."

Many seem never to consider that, while the punishment of an offender may have an influence over a non-offender, to deter him from an overt act of transgression, it may be doubted whether it has any influence on an old offender to lead him to repentance. Nor has it any influence to beget loving obedience (which alone is moral obedience), in the heart of any one, innocent or guilty. Hence it follows that, not only could none be recovered from guilt, who had transgressed; but that grateful obedience, which the redeemed sinner knows, would have been unknown. Even the obedience of angels is not prompted by gratitude. Justice deals out to them deserved reward. They know nothing of mercy, only as they see it shown towards fallen men. "Which things angels desire to look into." On this point, Mercy scores triumph No. 3.

(8) With these points gained, pardon is safe. The redeemed, the regenerated sinner is a more trustworthy citizen than the one who has never known the bitterness of condemnation and the inconceivable joy of salvation. He is safer, because a dread of sin itself, which is far more effectual than the dread of punishment, is begotten in the

depths of his soul. He knows the bitterness of the "fruit of the tree of the knowledge of good and evil," and wants no more of it. He is satisfied to feed henceforth on the fruit of the tree of life. Mercy's triumph No. 4.

(9) Multitudes are now saved, where all would, in all probability, have been lost. Had there been no offer of mercy, there would have been no hope in repentance, and hence no repentance. Despair is not capable of making a penitent plea, it excludes faith, and "without faith it is impossible to be well-pleasing unto him: for he that cometh to God must believe that he is, and that he is a rewarder of them that seek after him." Moreover, the nature of sin is to deceive the sinner as to the disposition of God towards him. Every man sees God through his own eyes. Ps. xviii. 25, 26, "With the merciful thou wilt show thyself merciful; with the perfect man thou wilt show thyself perfect; with the pure thou wilt show thyself pure; and with the perverse thou wilt show thyself froward." Under this delusion, hope of favor is impos-

sible; and application, supplication for mercy equally impossible. Here we find again the necessity for the gospel, what is termed "the means of grace." The revelations of the true attitude of God towards sinners, made by the advent, life, teaching, death, resurrection, and ascension of the Son of God, are the foundation of faith that the Father longs for, and will welcome, the return of his wandering and unhappy children. Hence, through the atonement, multitudes are now saved, where without it all would have been lost. Had the Creator foreseen such a result, of course the race would never have been created. This brings me to notice,

(10) This method of satisfying the demands of Justice by merciful means, and thus saving the sinner, was not an afterthought. It was part of the original plan, the culmination in fact of the whole plan of creation, as far as this world is concerned. The whole problem was fully solved, and each particular of the entire arrangement fully settled between the Father and the Word, who was in the beginning with God,

before "God created the heavens and the earth." The passages that seem to me to plainly teach this fact are, Rev. xiii. 8, "The Lamb slain from the foundation of the world;" I Peter i. 18-21. "Knowing that ye were redeemed, not with corruptible things, with silver or gold, from your vain manner of life, handed down from your fathers; but with precious blood, as of a lamb without blemish and without spot, even the blood of Christ; who was foreknown indeed before the foundation of the world, but was manifested at the end of the time for your sake, who through him are believers in God;" 2 Tim. i. 9, "According to his own purpose and grace, which was given us in Christ Jesus before times eternal." This idea is also sustained by the fact that the sacrifices required under the old dispensation were prophetic symbols of the atoning sacrifice, made in the fullness of time. If that event had not been prearranged, it could not have been predicted.

(11) In this arrangement, it is manifest that the Father, who planned all things, projected the scheme; and that the Son,

who has been the executive Deity from "the beginning," of his own free will, uninfluenced by any authority or compulsion, (except that moral compulsion that requires all intelligent beings, the infinite and the finite alike, to always act in view of the general good), consented to the arrangement, with full knowledge of all the self-sacrifice it would require, involving the necessity that he should assume the character of a man upon the earth, endure all the inconveniences of a mortal life under most distressing circumstances, be despised and rejected of men, suffer the agonies of Gethsemane and the cross, and spend a season in the tomb, to accomplish the great and wonderful end. This fact is particularly important, as refuting the disgraceful travesty, that has sometimes been advanced, that according to the atonement theory, God compelled his innocent Son to suffer and die under the penalty of the sins of others; thereby unjustly punishing the innocent and releasing the guilty. The fact that coercion of a moral agent is impossible, and the evidence that Jesus came on his mighty errand of his own free will, moved by the same love that moved the Father to send him, constitute a sufficient answer to all such carricature.

(12) It is often claimed that nothing was ever necessary, as a condition of pardon and restoration to the divine favor but repentance; and that, on that account, the doctrine of the necessity of an atonement is a myth. Such reasoners say, "God was always perfectly willing to forgive. He is not a wrathful, vengeful being; whose wrath must be appeased by a bloody, suffering sacrifice." The fallacy of this reasoning only lies in the fact that they have not taken all the facts into account in their premises. Recognizing only the fact that God did not require a bloody sacrifice to appease his wrath, and that he so loved the sinner that he would be glad to forgive him, and welcome him to all the joys of his loving favor and presence. They forget that the sinner himself has something to say in the case, that he may possibly refuse to accept any such gracious and loving offer.

We freely admit that God was always

willing and anxious to forgive. No bloody sacrifice was necessary to modify, in any respect, his attitude towards the sinner. It was the attitude of the sinner himself that needed to be changed. He it was who needed to be reconciled. He was at war against God, not God against him. The hindrance is not on God's part, that pardon is impossible where there is no penitence. The assumption that the sinner is ready, willing, anxious to be pardoned is a great mistake. Jesus says, "Ye will not come unto me that ye may have life." An edict of pardon can effect nothing, unless the offender will accept it. How can any man, how can God himself, compel an enemy to receive pardon? The necessity of the atonement was to bring the sinner to repentance, in other words to induce, persuade him to receive pardon.

Moreover, this theory is confronted by one of the most bald and extraordinary absurdities conceivable. It takes the government out of the hands of the Sovereign, and puts it into the hands of the offender himself. Repentance being the condition of pardon, and the offender being sovereign of his own volitions, he can remain in rebellion as long as he chooses, repent at the moment that suits him best, and compel the Executive to grant him a pardon, and release him from all liability to punishment, whenever he may be in the mood to do so. Would not that be a pretty state of things in a divine government, or any other? We should always bear in mind that it belongs to the government, not to offenders, to dictate terms of peace.

REMARKS.

1. This problem, how to deliver a culprit from the penalty of the law he had transgressed, and at the same time honor the government, shield the executive from censure, and give no encouragement to further disregard of the law, thus satisfying the last and least demand of Justice, was, so far as we are capable of judging, the greatest and most difficult ever submitted to and solved by the infinite mind. Its intricacy was so great that the discovery of the principle on which it was solved, even when the stupendous drama was enacted before our eyes,

has, until very recently, been impossible, even to the most careful and painstaking student. The reason is this. The details of the whole transaction are in perfect accordance with the principles of moral agency, and these are of recent discovery and, perhaps, only imperfectly understood, by the world's best thinkers, at the present time.

Viewed from the standpoint of the arbitrary Sovereignty of God, that solution was impossible. Hence the absurd hypotheses that have been advanced by which to reconcile the discrepancy between the necessity of executing the reasonable penalty of a righteous law, and the deliverance of a culprit, of whose guilt no possible doubt could be entertained, from that penalty, and restoring to him all the privileges and immunities of an unoffending citizen; and accomplishing this paradoxical feat of statesmanship in such a way as to secure the approbation of every citizen of the government, and reflect not even a shade of injustice upon the Sovereign.

2. What a misapprehension of the facts those have, who are ready to pluck the

Deity from his throne for creating men to send them to hell, when he knew beforehand that that would be the inevitable result. The true state of the case is, that multitudes are now saved, where all would have been lost; at least all who fell into sin; and those who are lost, go down to "the perdition of ungodly men" in spite of all the influences that infinite love could prompt, infinite wisdom devise, and infinite sacrifice execute and make efficient. Let men cease their complaining, fall in cheerfully with God's plan of a human life, accept the responsibilities of moral agency, and gain the glorious condition thus made possible to them, and all will be well. God will be honored, and man attain to the glories of an immortal and eternal existence of happiness ineffable.

3. A moment's reflection will show how immeasurably the guilt of the finally incorrigible will be enhanced by their persistence in sin, against the unexampled and persistent means of grace that they reject and despise. The justice of their final doom will be acquiesced in and approved by all, the

saved and the lost, when the revelations of the final judgment shall correct the errors, clear away the mist, and rectify the fallacious reasoning of those who now "complain against God."

4. The Jews in their rejection and crucifiction of the Son of God, and all incorrigible sinners no less, in their refusal to accept him as their Savior, have made, and do continually make, such an exhibition of the nature and consequent desert of sin as will forever exclude them from all pity. Criminals never receive moral approval and support from any quarter, not even from their own companions in crime. How can they when they are condemned of their own consciences? He who can not approve his own conduct should not, and need not, expect approval from any person, in heaven or on earth. In proof of this, ask each one of a gang of desperadoes what he thinks of his companions in crime, taking them one by one, and he will say of each, "He is a hard case."

There is no other aspect of sin in which it appears so heinous, so cruel, so unreasonable, so heartless, so inhuman, so hateful, so mean, as when it rages angrily, maliciously, boisterously, against innocence, against kindness, against love, against self-sacrifice for the raging sinner himself. What a scene was that when the raving crowd cried out, "Away with him! Crucify him!" and Pilate asked, "Why? what evil hath he done?" Sure enough. How pertinent the inquiry, "Why? what evil hath he done?" The spotless Lamb of God "came unto his own, and his own received him not." Was it not this exhibition of this deep depravity, the inexpressible ingratitude of the incorrigible sinner, that wrung the sweat from his very veins, in the garden of Gethsemane? Verily, verily, there is no other form in which sin appears so exceedingly sinful as when the sinner deliberately rejects the merciful offer of salvation, as it is presented in the atoning blood, that is, in the suffering life and cruel death on Calvary, of Jesus, the Son of God.

5. One thought more, before we close this already protracted discussion. This is the particular doctrine in which lies "the

power of God unto salvation." Men will never forsake sin with resolute purpose, and successfully, and avail themselves of divine help to that end, until they realize the hatefulness, the exceeding sinfulness of sin; and this a mere exemplary and sympathizing Christ can never beget. It is the self-sacrificing, suffering, dying Christ, who makes the sinner ashamed of his alienation, and causes him to long for reconciliation. "We love him because he first loved us."

Ministers who leave the doctrine of the atonement out of their sermons, and endeavor to make men Christlike by portraying his perfect, unselfish life, as an example and high model, to be admired and imitated, need not wonder that few, or none, are converted under their preaching. How shall men be persuaded to sincerely and earnestly make Christ their model, who do not even follow the example and adopt the maxims of the living Christian men and women with whom they daily associate? Depend upon it, the gospel that saves is not Christ our model, but Christ the crucified. The cross; that is, the atoning sacrifice of him, "who his own self bare our sins in his body upon the tree," is the central sun of the gospel system, around which every other gospel truth revolves, as a planet in its orbit.

Many will tell me they do not understand this doctrine, and how can they teach it? To this question I have two answers. First, you may not understand the chemistry of water or of food, yet you can give water to the thirsty and food to the hungry. "Preach the word;" and leave the rest with God. My second answer is, Study it until you do understand it; and then preach it, until your hearers understand it. The explanation, the philosophy of the atonement, as given in this course of lectures, is not difficult to understand. There are many problems whose solution is very difficult; but, when solved, the solution is so simple that everybody wonders why he did not solve it himself. It was easy for the royal court of Spain to stand an egg on its end, after Columbus had shown how it could be done. The true philosophy of the atonement has waited long for the true philosophy of moral agency. When men acquaint themselves with the latter, they will find it easy to comprehend the former. Do not rest, my reader, until you see clearly that the Love of God, in the gift of his Son, and the Love of the Son, in voluntarily laying down his life for the sinner, answer the end and purpose of the penalty of the law, in the case of all who believe, more perfectly and satisfactorily even to justice itself than the execution of that penalty could have done; and that the very highest desires of Mercy are realized at the same time: Justice heartily consenting that the truly penitent shall be pardoned and saved; and Mercy as heartily consenting that the penalty of the law shall be executed on those who will not repent.

LECTURE VII.

REGENERATION—CONVERSION.

This subject is another dark place on which light is needed. Some there are who have quite well-defined views on the subject, but very erroneous; a few have well-defined views, that are in the main correct; but a very large majority, even of the clergy, only "see men as trees walking," when they turn their intellectual eyes upon it. The result is that, in many pulpits, the subject is never mentioned at all; in many others, it is referred to only to " darken counsel by words without knowledge;" and in a few, it is intelligently, but usually only partially handled. The truth is, it is a question, like that of the atonement, that can never be clearly understood only in the light of a correct philosophy of moral agency.

The words regeneration and conversion are generally supposed to be synonymous. My opinion is that, while the difference is not of such a nature as to necessitate fundamental error, it may be the occasion of an error that is, to say the least, very serious. The words are very far from being synonymous in their etymology. Regeneration, etymologically, means begotten again, or born again. The word conversion contains no hint of either begetting or birth, either in the Latin from which the word is derived, or in the Greek from which it is translated. Its idea is simply that of turning around. Words that differ so widely in their literal signification have no rightful claim to being synonymous. To my mind it is very clear that regeneration refers particularly to the begetting and bringing into being a new inward life. This is the work of the Holy Spirit. Conversion, turning around, facing the other way, is the act of the sinner himself. It is he who says, "I will arise and go to my father;" "Lord, what wilt thou have me to do?" This difference will be further elucidated as we proceed with this discussion.

My object in this lecture is to trace, as minutely as possible, each step in this important change. That we may do this intelligently, we purpose to turn upon the subject the light of the scriptures, the light of philosophy, and the light of experience. Let us consider,

1. The state, the moral condition, of the unregenerate man.

The most minute photograph of such a person that perhaps has ever been taken is found in Rom. 1:28–32. "As they refused to have God in their knowledge, God gave them up unto a reprobate mind, to do those things that are not fitting; being filled with all unrighteousness, wickedness, covetousness, maliciousness; full of envy, murder, strife, deceit, malignity; whisperers, backbiters, haters of God, insolent, haughty, boastful, inventors of evil things, disobedient to parents, without understanding, covenant-breakers, without natural affection, unmerciful; who knowing the ordinance of God, that they who practice such things are worthy of death, not only do the same, but also consent with them that practice them." Many other passages though not so extensive in their particulars, are equally explicit, as to the shockingly depraved and deplorable condition to which sin degrades the human soul. See also 2 Pet. ii. 10-15.

The philosophy of moral agency, sustained also by scripture, presents the case in this way. Man is tripartite. (See Lecture II.) He is constituted of soul, body and spirit. The soul is the inner man, the real man, the man himself. It is the soul that says I, I am, I think, I feel, I will. The body is the medium through which the soul holds communion with the material world. The spirit in the medium through which the soul holds communion with the spirit-world. The sinner is the bondservant of the flesh. John viii. 34, "Every one that committeth sin is the bondservant of sin." Rom. vi. 16, "To whom ye present yourselves as bondservants unto obedience, his bondservants ye are whom ye obey." Rom. viii. 6, "The minding of the flesh is death." Rom. viii. 7, "The minding of the flesh is enmity against God." This bondage, though contracted voluntarily and continued voluntarily, allbeit the judgment disapproves and the conscience is far from being quiet, is the most gauling, abject and tyrannical known.

Rom. vii. 15, 18, 19, 22–24, "Not what I would, that do I practice; but what I hate, that do I. In my flesh dwelleth no good thing; for to will is present with me, but to do that which is good is not. For the good which I would I do not; but the evil which I would not, that I practice. For I delight in the law of God after the inward man; but I see a different law in my members, warring against the law of my mind, and bringing me into captivity under the law of sin which is in my members. "O, wretched man that I am! who shall deliver me out of the body of this death?" This language is very strong, but I apprehend it does not overstate the facts in the case. The repeated failures of those who undertake their own reformation, as well as the oft repeated confession, "I cannot break myself of this bad habit," are strongly confirmatory of a state of things that is in the highest degree deplorable. The apostle Paul says, Gal. v. 17, "The flesh lusteth against the spirit and the spirit against the flesh; for these are contrary the one to the other; so that ye may not do the things that ye would."

These passages, and there are others to the same import, clearly represent a state of inability that is with difficulty reconcilable with the voluntary and accountable condition of the wretched sinner, in this state of bondage. To admit that he cannot escape would be admitting that he is no longer accountable, no longer sinful, for remaining in it; no longer a moral agent. This will never do. If that is the case, you may as well proclaim the gospel to the beasts of the field as to him. My solution of the difficulty is this. I admit the full force of the declaration of the sinner's inability, as found in these passages; but I claim that while he may not be able, in and of himself, to break the gauling chains of the miserable death in which he is bound and in which he groans, he is still able to "lay hold of the hope set before us" in the gospel. Though dead, life is within his reach. "God hath given to us eternal life, and that life is in his Son;" and that Son stands by his side, able and willing to speak the life-giving word, whenever he will lend a willing ear. A drowning man may be unable to climb upon the deck of a passing vessel and save himself; but he may still be able to seize a rope that is thrown to him and be lifted safely to the deck by another. If he refuse to avail himself of this proffered assistance, he alone is responsible. He will remain in his perishing condition voluntarily. Thus the inability of the sinner to deliver himself from his bondage does not excuse him for perishing. If he perish, it will be because he will not choose to be saved. The Savior is within his reach; he has but to look and live.

2. Every one must see, at a glance, that this state of heart and mode of life "must" be changed, before there can be any happiness or even peace to such a character. "The wicked are like the troubled sea; for it cannot rest, and its waters cast up mire and dirt. There is no peace, saith my God, to the wicked." It was for this reason that Jesus said, "Ye must be born again."

3. It is also manifest that the change to be wrought, effecting a reconciliation between God, man's Father and Sovereign,

and men individually, who are in this state of alienation and rebellion, must take place in the rebel, not in his Lord and King. The government must announce the conditions of reconciliation; and the rebel must comply with them. The sinner must become reconciled to God, not God to the sinner.

4. God, as head of the government, realizing the helplessness and hopelessness, as well as the stubbornness and pride of the sinner, having also a father's anxiety for his welfare and happiness, in addition to having already satisfied Justice through the atoning sacrifice, takes the initiative, in effecting his practical reformation, by first issuing his proclamation of pardon to all who will lay down the arms of their rebellion, and humbly, and penitently take the oath of allegiance; and secondly, by the work of the Holy Spirit. 1 Pet. 1.3, "Blessed be the God and Father of our Lord Jesus Christ, who according to his great mercy begat us again unto a living hope."

5. In the regeneration of the heart of the sinner, the first practical act is the be-

getting of a new life by the Spirit. The first meaning of the word *gennao* is to beget. It is found forty-one times in the first sixteen verses of the first chapter of Mathew's gospel, and frequently in other places in the New Testament. When fatherhood is referred to, this is the word universally used. In the passive voice, it also means to be born. In this usage it applies to motherhood. In recognition of this begetting, theologians, up to quite recently, held that the whole process of regeneration was effected in the hearts of those who were predestinated to be saved; and that the sinner could do nothing towards his own salvation until this regeneration was thus effected. As soon as the philosophy of moral agency came to be better understood, the impossibility of this hypothesis became apparent, and the doctrine was rejected, yielding place, however to another error, not quite so repulsive, but still failing to account for all the phenomena frequently manifest at this point of the sinner's experience.

Many persons who have been converted, and many others, who have not been converted, have been conscious of a quickening of their moral sensibilities, at times and under circumstances that rendered it impossible to trace their origin to any other than a spiritual source. This has occurred both in Christian and in heathen lands. Men and women, who were far removed from all Christian influences, and had for years known no serious impressions of a religious nature, have suddenly experienced such an awakening of conscience, and realized such a consciousness of their accountability to God, and their sinfulness in his sight, as gave them no rest day nor night, until they went to him with their burden, sought his pardoning grace, and covenanted with him to lead a new life. Several instances of this kind have come under my own personal observation; and missionaries among idolatrous heathen have found cases of a similar awakening among those who have never heard of salvation through the Christian's Savior and the Christian's God.

Now, although positive proof-texts on this point are few, collateral evidence, both scriptural and rational, besides the experiences mentioned above, are abundant. The fact that the prodigal son, "came to himself" is no evidence that the Holy Spirit did not use his starving, wretched, degraded condition, as means to awaken in his soul the realization of his folly and wickedness, and thus prompt the remembrance of the pleasant home of his father, where there "was bread enough and to spare." No new facts had come to his knowledge. These thoughts had, undoubtedly, often crossed his mind before. Why did they impress him so deeply at that time as to conquer his pride, and make him willing to humbly confess, "Father, I have sinned, and am no more worthy to be called thy son!" Was there nothing supernatural about this?

Again, is not this "just like God?" Did he not send his Son "to seek and to save that which was lost?" and when the Son left the world, did he not tell his disciples, "It is expedient for you that I go away; for if I go not away, the Comforter will not come unto you; but if I go, I will send him unto you?" Now, if the Savior came to seek the lost, and if the presence of the Comforter, "which is the Holy Spirit," is better for the world than the personal presence of the Son, must he not be engaged in the same work of seeking the lost? and if he seeks the lost, is it not he who first quickens in the heart of the sinner the germs of a new life? "You did he quicken (make alive) when ye were dead through your trespasses and sins." "God, when we were dead through our trespasses, quickened us." "Dead!" Can the dead bring themselves to life? and can they do anything until they are made alive?

One consideration more. Jesus said, "No man can come to me, except the Father that sent me draw him.' "No man!" This must include sinners of every period of time and of every part of the earth—all sinners. Now, if a divine influence is necessary to induce a sinner to come to Christ, what is that influence, if it be not of the Holy Spirit? and, if such an influence must be exerted upon the sinner to bring him to Christ, when shall it be exerted, if not as the initiatory act of his coming? This conclusion is still further confirmed by another passage that is directly and positively to the point: "And he (the Comforter), when he is come, will convict the world in respect of sin." This must refer to what has always been known as conviction of sin, and which every regenerated person knows as the initial experience, leading the entire procession of experiences through which he or she was led in passing "from darkness to light, and from the power of Satan unto God."

In view of all these considerations, and more might be mentioned, we believe we are safe in maintaining that there is no other influence in the world that is able to beget in the sinful soul that "Godly sorrow, that worketh repentance unto salvation." Many are the means that the Spirit employs, as instruments to this end, and that are usually the only means recognized by the sinner; but, though they had often been impressed upon the mind before, they were never effectual until that special, favored time. It was then the Spirit of the Lord that emphasized the preached word, an exhortation, a prayer, a convert's testimony, an affliction, a remarkable escape from danger or death, and fastened it "as a nail in a sure place," giving the soul no rest until repentance and regeneration were complete.

This discussion has been somewhat protracted, though not more so than its importance demands, but we cannot leave it until we add that this conviction is not special; that is, it is not confined to those who yield to it and are saved. Jesus said, "I am the light of the world." John said, "That was the true light that lighteth every man that cometh into the world," and since he "tasted death for every man," and since the Spirit is pushing to completion the work he inaugurated, it must be that no one is left unwarned. I believe that even heathen, who have no knowledge of Christ as the Savior of the world, or of the true God, are often touched by a conscience that is quickened by the Holy Spirit. Thus the initiatory step, or act, in the regeneration of the sinner, is the quickening of conscience by the Holy Spirit.

6. The second step, or act, in this extraordinary work, is by the sinner himself.

This is the most critical moment of his life. His conduct, at this juncture, will, in all probability, determine his destiny. I do not say he never will have another call, but I do say he may not. The issue is whether he will heed this warning, whether he will encourage this germ of a new life, by thoughtful attention, conscientious consideration of the facts in the case, and pursue the course of wisdom and reason; or whether he will banish thought, smother that life-germ, resist the Spirit, harden his heart, and plunge into a deeper depravity of soul and a more reckless course of life than he ever knew before. If he will be saved, now is the time to "make his calling and election sure." God elects those to be saved who elect him, choose Christ to be their Savior. This is the moment for that choice. "I will arise and go to my Father."

7. Precisely at this juncture, if the person has been properly instructed, will occur that penitence, that "Godly sorrow," that is of such vital importance, in securing a genuine work of grace in the heart. It is seriously to be feared that a large percent-

age of the evangelistic work that has been done in these later years has been deficient at this point. The "exceeding sinfulness of sin" has received but little attention. The young want to be saved, of course; everybody wants to be saved; and they are told to take Christ for their Savior. To this they assent, and are then assured that they are saved. Not one word is spoken about sin; not a word about a confession; they are not even told to pray, to "call upon the name of the Lord" that they may be saved; to cry out, like the publican, "God be merciful to me, a sinner." When we inquire respecting "penitential tears," we are told these have never committed any great crimes. It is not to be expected that they will feel the sense of sin that an old and hardened offender would. Now, I pronounce all that a fearful if not a fatal delusion. If there is any such thing as "daubing with untempered mortar; crying peace, peace, when their is no peace," I am sure that is it. The most amiable and unoffending child in the world, if properly instructed, will realize a state of mind and heart, for which it will feel deep penitence, "Godly sorrow, that worketh repentance unto salvation." An amiable disposition is not a Christian heart and purpose. Every soul "must be born again." Take Jesus' word for that; and neither delude yourself nor others. "If the blind guide the blind, both shall fall into a pit." Too great stringency on that point is better than too great laxity. It is a sense of sinfulness, contrasted with the pure and perfect holiness of God, that humbles and subdues the soul, and makes it like that of "a little child."

It is to be deplored that this subduing and contrition of the heart does not always occur at this point as it should. This is the beginning of the end. Softening and hardening originate at the same point, and this is the point. This is the first question to be decided by the sinner, Will I yield, or will I resist? For the yielding, or the stubborn hardening of the will, at this point, the individual alone is responsible. Here he enters "the straight gate that leadeth to life," or continues in "the broad way that leadeth to destruction."

8. Repentance is next in order. What is it?

This word occurs frequently, both in the Old and New Testament, still there is scarcely another word respecting whose exact meaning and use, in this cennection, there is so much confusion. Most people suppose it to mean penitence, as defined above. This is a great mistake. The word *metanoia*, found twenty-four times in the New Testament, and translated repentance every time, contains, etymologically, no intimation of penitence. Its literal signification is a change of mind, a change of purpose; and this is its uniform meaning in the New Testament. When it is used in connection with no word that signifies sorrow, that idea may be implied, since sorrow for a wrong course of life must naturally precede a turning from it; but no hint of penitence is contained in the word itself. Using the word in this sense, the forming of a new purpose is the step next in order, after coming to one's self and realizing the folly, the wickedness, of one's previous life. The purpose formed is, "I will arise and go to my Father." By the grace of God, I must, I will forsake my sins and lead a new life. Henceforth God shall be my King, and his will shall be the law of my life.

This is the strongest, the most solemn, the most unalterable vow the soul ever makes or can ever make. No other contract, or agreement, known among men, is so unalterable as this. Its import is, "I have opened my mouth unto the Lord, and I cannot go back." Evangelists should make note of this, and should give clear, positive instruction upon this point, made emphatic by oft repetition. Partnerships, business engagements, contracts among men, even the sacred oath of marriage, may, for sufficient reason, be annulled; but this never. No sufficient reason can ever be found for annulling the soul's oath of allegiance to God. That vow can never be broken, except at the expense of great guilt.

9. Immediately following this change of purpose, repentance, comes the earnest prayer for pardon. The promise is, "Whosoever shall call upon the name of the Lord

shall be saved." The prayer is, "God be merciful to me a sinner;" "Lord save me, I perish;" "Lord, what wilt thou have me to do?" The acceptable prayer, at this point, must include three things: confession, which implies penitence; supplication for pardon; and submission to the will of God, which is the oath of loyal allegiance. These are the only conditions on which any government, human or divine, can safely listen to a prayer for pardon. Thus it is that "Godly sorrow worketh repentance unto salvation."

I cannot pass this point without adding another important suggestion to those who are endeavoring to point the sinner to "the Lamb of God, that taketh away the sin of the world." Tell such a soul to pray, to pray aloud, whether in secret or in public. Ordinarily no other instruction is necessary. The penitent who prays, and prays earnestly and persistently, will find the light; and when he has found it, it will be "the true light.". Instruction of any other kind is only necessary, when the soul has fallen into a snare. The soul that prays will usually trust. If it does not, then instruct it on that point, but not until then. The usual custom of instructing inquirers to "trust Jesus," without knowing whether they are in a penitent, repentant or prayerful state of mind, will only at best, "heal the hurt of the daughter of my people slightly," where they should be and may be healed fully and soundly.

10. Answer to prayer. No further progress can be made in this succession of events, until this prayer is answered. Should pardon of past sins be denied, hope and faith would expire together, and eternal despair take their place. This, however, is an impossibility, under the circumstances supposed. No sincere, earnest prayer can be righteously spurned by a government that has promised pardon, when the conditions of such pardon have been fully and honestly complied with. No sooner does the prayer "God be merciful to me a sinner" go up from a sincere heart than the edict goes forth, "Thy sins are forgiven thee; go in peace and sin no more."

11. Now is the time for faith; that is, now is the time to speak of faith, to make

faith a specialty. Penitent for sin; fully resolved on reformation of life; realizing his unworthiness and helplessness; yielding his will to the will of God; he may now confidently "trust Jesus." Now he may plead the promises, "Him that cometh to me, I will in no wise cast out;" "If we confess our sins, he is faithful and righteous to forgive us our sins, and to cleanse us from all unrighteousness."

Let me add at this point, this is by no means the first exercise of faith, on the part of the sinner. At each step of this series of experiences through which he has passed, he has exercised faith, but at each step faith in a different thing. First he believed he was a sinner; then he believed that God is merciful, and that penitence is acceptable to him; then that it would not be a vain and fruitless act to repent; then he hoped, at least, that God would hear his earnest, penitent prayer; now he hears, by the ear of faith, the voice of the Savior saying, "Thy sins are forgiven thee; go in peace and sin no more." This is the cosummating act of faith on his part.

At this point faith seems to be more important and worthy of special mention, because it is exercised at the moment of his greatest extremity, when temptation to doubt and despair is greatest. The sense of his sinfulness and unworthiness has been growing more and more intense as the work of reformation has progressed, until he now realizes that it will require a miracle of mercy to save him. Like Paul, he thinks himself the chief of sinners. Can he now believe that "whosoever" can possibly be made to include him? Hence his cry is the wail of expiring hope, "Lord save or I perperish." Under these circumstances, faith means something, and is worthy of special mention. The Savior seems to say just then, "Be it unto thee according to thy faith." "All things are possible to him that believeth." The response of faith is, "Lord I believe;" and immediately the billows of fearful emotion that have agitated his soul subside. Peace reigns. "Being justified by faith, we have peace with God through our Lord Jesus Christ." The sinner is born again. The atonement is now complete. He is reconciled to God.

11. The witness of the Spirit. The significance of the witness of the Spirit, at this point, is very great. The experience through which the soul has just passed is the most extraordinary ever known to man. It is not a trifling matter to be raised from death to life; to be "delivered out of the power of darkness, and translated into the kingdom of God's dear Son." The power of "the prince of this world" has been broken, but the tempter is still lingering around. The soul that was "a cage of unclean birds" is "swept and garnished," but it is "empty." The great question at this moment is, Shall the demon that has just been cast out return and, finding the soul unoccupied, "with seven other spirits more evil than himself, enter in and dwell there?" or shall the high purpose of the soul be strengthened by a voice within witnessing with his spirit that he is a child of God? The soul that is just entering upon its regenerated life should never rest satisfied until the witness of the spirit is clear, and it is able

to "rejoice in hope of the glory of God." Evangelists and pastors should be more particular at this point than they usually are. The steps of progress, as described in Rom. v. 1, 2, are first peace, then steadfastness, then joy in hope, which is followed, when stronger grown, by joy "in tribulations also." " Being justified by faith we have peace with God through our Lord Jesus Christ; through whom also we have had our access by faith into this grace wherein we stand; and we rejoice in hope of the glory of God."

Such, or similar to these, are the experiences by which the soul is exercised, with more or less distinctness according to the temperament of the person and the degree of intelligence with which he observes the exercises of his own mind, in passing from death into life; the whole constituting the change, the experience, that is properly and truly called REGENERATION.

12. Lest I should be misunderstood respecting the universality of the recognition of each step of this experience, as given above, let me say, I believe there are many

in these days, and probably always have been, who are led to accept Christ as their Savior, and enter into acceptable relations with him, in whose experiences these successive steps are not all distinctly marked. This is owing, not so much to the absence of the facts as to a difference in the power and habit of introspection. Some people seem to take no cognizance of the phenomena of their own minds, while others allow no important mental change to occur without their notice. This difference lies in their constitutions and habits. In every case of true regeneration, however, these steps will be taken, whether observed or not.

13. A few words now respecting conversion will close this elaborate discussion. Conversion, as stated at the outset, means a turning around. It may refer, in part, to the acts of penitence and repentence already mentioned, performed by the convicted soul, but its chief application is to the change that takes place in the outward life of one who has experienced regeneration. This change, as is well known, is often very marked, and always more or less observable.

Even when deportment seemed as perfect as a human life could well be, before regeneration, a marked change will be observable in the spirit, the heart with which everything is done. Regeneration is the change of heart; conversion the change of the outward life.

LECTURE VIII.

ANGELS.

Wherever in the universe of God there are intelligent beings, they are and must be moral agents. The only class of finite beings, outside of our own race, of which we have any well-defined knowledge, is the angels. Of cherubim and seraphim we have but little idea. Whether they differ from angels so radically as to constitute them a different order of intelligences, we do not know. One thing we do know, however; if they are intelligent beings, endowed with the power of choice under an alternative, they are moral agents, and must be subject to all the conditions of the angels.

Our first inquiry is, Who are the angels?

1. A very common misapprehension, doubtless of long standing, is that the angels are the souls of mortals who have departed this life. This is a grave and by no means a harmless mistake. A few years ago the children of our Sunday-Schools

were taught to sing, "I want to be an angel." It was wrong. Men, women and children will never be angels; nor will angels ever be mortal.

2. Angels are a distinct class of intelligent beings, finite but not mortal. By what means they were brought into existence, or of what substance they were created, is not even hinted in the scriptures. "They neither marry, nor are given in marriage," nor are they subject to death; hence their number was permanently fixed from the time of their creation.

3. Scripture allusions to them are numerous; and it is clearly intimated that their creation antedated that of man, and probably antedated the creation of the material universe. When "Jehovah answered Job out of the whirlwind," speaking of the time when the foundations of the earth were laid, he says, (Job xxxviii, 7), "Who laid the corner stones thereof, when the morning stars sang together, and all the sons of God shouted for joy?" These "morning stars" that sang together, and the "sons of God" who "shouted for joy" could have

been no beings of whom we have knowledge, unless they were the angels. Of the many facts to which we might call attention respecting the angels, we have to do only, or mainly, with those that relate to them as moral agents.

4. The angelic hosts are all moral agents. All the conditions of moral agency: intelligence, free will and opportunity, are theirs. As to the degree of their intelligence; though we have no direct and positive information on the subject, we are probably justified in presuming that it is superior to that of man. It would not be natural to suppose that the beings who were created expressly to be God's messengers to men, would be an inferior grade of intelligences. We read of "the angels that excel in strength." Doubtless this does not refer to physical strength alone, if indeed, it refers to it at all, but to superior might in every respect.

The following argument is also clearly legitimate in regard to them. A finite mind knows nothing it has not learned, either by tuition, intuition or logical deduction.

When it comes into being, it is an utter blank. It knows nothing. At any subsequent period of its existence, the degree of its intelligence will be determined by the natural capacity with which it is endowed by the Creator, plus the amount it has learned, up to that time. Now, whatever may have been the natural capacity for intelligence, with which angels were originally endowed, they have had ages of tuition and experience, that long before this time has given them a mental development and amount of information utterly inconceivable to us. Their degree of intelligence at the present time, however, has nothing to do with the question of their moral agency. If, when they were created, they were capable of learning by precept, and understanding a command and the nature of an obligation, that is sufficient to fulfil the first condition of moral agency.

The second condition, freedom of choice, the sovereign exercise of the will-power, is manifest from every fact we know respecting them, and will be abundantly apparent as we proceed. Of their opportunities, nothing seems necessary to be said. The power of choice, in the presence of a command to do or not to do, supplies all the necessary conditions of will in liberty, and necessitates moral action and moral character. Their alternative, like ours, is loyalty or disloyalty to God, their Creator and Sovereign. In this respect, they do not differ from men; but their loyalty or disloyalty will manifest itself under different circumstances. Its test may not be the gratification of a fleshly appetite, like that of Adam in the garden, or Jesus in the wilderness; but it may be ambition for preference or power, or a suggestion of presumption.

5. The sad fact is very apparent that a large number of these first created, highly endowed, favorably situated "morning stars" "kept not their own principality, but left their proper habitation," and are "kept in everlasting bonds under darkness unto the judgment of the great day." Such an event is possible only to moral agents. Angels sinned, and, like other sinners, are under condemnation, "condemned already."

6. What the form of temptation was,

the form in which the great alternative came to them, is not stated in the scriptures; but to human reason there appears one form most probable, and, so far as I know, but one form has ever been suggested. That form is ambition. The second form in which temptation came to our Savior was the promise that the kingdoms of the world and the glory of them should be his, if he would worship, that is, exalt as supreme, Satan instead of God. This would naturally be the first appeal to disloyalty that would be presented to an intelligence not encumbered with the flesh, and having no fleshly appetites to gratify.

Among the angels, as among men, there are undoubtedly different degrees of intelligence. Some have learned more than others. Some may have been more highly endowed than others; we cannot tell. Hence, some are superior to others in rank. Jude tells us of "Michael, the archangel." Daniel also says that Michael "is the great prince," and again, "one of the princes," which would plainly intimate that there are several princes, and that they hold different grades. One ranks higher than another. Gabriel is mentioned under such circumstances as to plainly intimate that he also is one of the arch-angels, if not at the head of the whole angelic host. It was he who was commissioned to announce to Mary that she, of all the virgins of Israel, was chosen to be the mother of Jesus, the Savior of the world, the son of God. It would seem to be reasonable to suppose that the very chief of all the heavenly messengers would be sent on this greatest of all the missions on which angels could be employed.

It matters not to us which of these may have held precedence, or whether there was yet another, who was at one time of still higher rank than they were, but who distinguished himself in a transaction so shameful, so disgraceful, so harmful withall to the rest and to us, that the lofty appellation by which he may have been first known, has never been revealed to us; but who is known to us by a name most appropriate, most expressive of his diabolical history. That detestable name is *ho diabolos* the devil, also called Satan. He is also designated by many other dishonorable epithets.

It is, then, but natural, that is, according to the nature of a finite mind, that, finding himself thus endowed with ability and influence superior to the rest of the angelic host, he should deem it his right, or, at least, that it was gratifying to his ambition, to assume authority over them; and finding this disapproved by him, "whose right it is" to rule, he should attempt to subvert his government, and enthrone himself supreme. This view of the case, taken in connection with his free agency, and with the same freedom of choice on the part of all the rest of the angelic host, will fully account for the fact that he should first rebel, then lead astray a large multitude, though but a small part, of the inferior grade of angels. This is the way such things work among men; why not among angels? These constitute "the devil and his angels."

A sufficiently full account of the fall of the angels to suggest to a thinker the real nature and result of this rebellion is found in Rev. xii. 7–9. The war in heaven there described was, as is generally assumed, a contention that arose for supremacy, in which Michael and his angels were loyal to God, and contended against "the dragon and his angels," finally overcoming them, and forcing them with their intrigues out of the holy city. "The great dragon was cast down, the old serpent, that is called the Devil and Satan, the deceiver of the whole world; he was cast down to the earth, and his angels were cast down with him."

7. We have, then, two classes of angels; the Holy Angels and the Fallen Angels. What are their employments?

(1) The holy angels are "ministering spirits, sent forth to do service for the sake of them that shall inherit salvation." Instances of this angelic service are found recorded in the Scriptures, from the days of Abraham to the close of the revelation made to John on the Isle of Patmos; and who can find evidence that their ministrations are not just as common since as they were during all that period? Several passages re-

specting them plainly intimate that they belong to every age, and to the people of God in all lands. Speaking of children, Jesus says, "Their angels do always behold the face of my Father who is in heaven;" and David says "The angel of Jehovah encampeth round about them that fear him, and delivereth them."

(2) The fallen angels were "cast down to the earth," "having great wrath," "to deceive the nations that are in the four corners of the earth." This seems to have been their business from the time the serpent beguiled Eve in the garden of Eden until the present; and doubtless will be until they are "cast into the lake of fire and brimstone," at "the judgment of the great day."

8. Here we are brought again face to face with certain questions of great moment, that have long puzzled honest and earnest inquirers, and have furnished the devil a standing place, from which many a successful attack has been made against the truth, the church, and the cause of righteousness. It is for the very purpose of giving positive, truthful, and I hope final answers to this

class of question, answers that are sustained by both Scripture and philosophy, that I have undertaken the writing of these lectures. The doctrine of moral agency furnishes the key that unlocks and throws wide open the portals of the dark chamber in which most of these mysteries have been hidden for ages, and brings to light the glittering, blazing diamonds of truth, whose existence has been long suspected, but never satisfactorily and positively proven. The questions that I shall present are not all of this character. The answers to some of them have always been plain enough, but are now made more positive and indisputable than ever before.

Respecting the fallen angels, we note the following:

(1) Is the devil, and are his angels, actual, living, thinking, choosing, planning personalities?

My answer to this question is positively, unhesitatingly, indubitably, Yes! but let that pass. The proper way to instruct those who ask questions is to lead them to the facts that will enable them to see the answers themselves. When one answers his own question, he is much more likely to be satisfied with the answer than when he takes the *ipse dixit* of the best teacher in the world.

Let us read together Dan. viii. 15-19. "Behold there stood before me as the appearance of a man. And I heard a man's voice between the banks of Ulai, which called, and said, Gabriel, make this man to understand the vision. So he came near where I stood; and when he came I was afraid and fell upon my face; but he said unto me, Understand, O son of man; for at the time of the end shall be the vision. Now as he was speaking with me, I was in a deep sleep on my face toward the ground; but he touched me and set me upright. And he said, Behold I will make thee know what shall be in the last end of the indignation." What think you? was this "appearance of a man," whose name was Gabriel, who talked intelligently with Daniel, who touched him and set him upright—was this man an actual personality, or was it a myth, a fancy, a dream? An examination of the context, in which this passage is found, will show that this was no part of Daniel's vision. It was an open-face reality, giving him an understanding of a vision that he had seen, and of which he had "sought for the meaning."

Several other passages might be referred to; but one is sufficient. Let us read Luke i. 26: "The angel Gabriel was sent from God unto a city of Galilee, named Nazareth." This angel Gabriel talked with the virgin Mary, and told her that she would be the mother of Jesus, who should "be called the Son of the Most High," and who should "reign over the house of Jacob forever." Is there any doubt of the personality of Gabriel in these transactions? Is there any doubt of the personality of "Michael the archangel, when contending with the devil he disputed about the body of Moses" (Jude 9)? In fact, is there any doubt that all the holy angels are living, intelligent beings, persons? It would be difficult for one who has any idea of moral agency to conceive of a "holy" being who is not an intelligent person; and it is equally impossible to conceive of an unholy, that is a wicked, being who is not an intelligent person. If the holy angels are persons, are not the fallen angels persons too? If these were persons before they fell, are they not persons still? and will they not always be persons? The truth is, there is no notion with which skeptical minds have befogged their own intelligence and reason, that is more unreasonable and absurd than that demons are not actual, living, intelligent persons. Listen then seriously, soberly, rationally, diligently, to the warning of Peter (1 Pet. v. 8), "Be sober, be watchful; your adversary, the devil, as a roaring lion, walketh about, seeking whom he may devour: whom withstand steadfast in your faith." With this idea of personality, every mention of the devil and demons, in the Scriptures, is in perfect harmony. Not an idea of any thing else is even fairly inferable, in a single instance. The truth is, "He was a murderer from the beginning, and standeth not in the truth, because there is no truth in him. When he speaketh a lie, he speaketh of his own; for he is a liar and the father thereof;" and this idea, that there is no personal devil, is one of his most absurd, not even plausible, lies. Disbelief in a personal devil is the first step on the shortest road to Atheism. The assumption is just as groundless and unreasonable as the assumption that there is no God.

(2.) Another silly, unreasoning question, often asked, is, Who made the devil? The philosophy of moral agency answers this question also. With equal pertinence and propriety we may ask, Who made all the bad men, who have cursed the world since the day when Cain lifted murderous hands upon his brother? Who made Guiteau, the murderer of President Garfield? He was once an innocent babe in the arms of a loving mother, a God-given child, yet God did not make him a murderer. So God made the angels innocent, and each one became loyal and holy, or disloyal and unholy, in the exercise of his own power of choice. These latter we call devils, demons, fiends, and such they are, but by no fault of their Maker. Their leader is *ho diabolos*, the devil; "his angels" are properly called demons, *daimonia*, or *daimones*.

(3.) We read that "all things work together for good to them that love God;" what good was accomplished by this apostacy of angels and war in heaven? To this question we answer, Every moral agent must be tested, in order that he may form a fixed character. As the result of this testing of the loyalty of the angels, those who refused to be led away from their loyalty to God are now firmly fixed in their purpose of loyalty. Hence they are called holy angels. They have a fixed and reliable character. Now they can be trusted anywhere. No influence in the universe can dissuade them from their purpose. They have passed through the severest test they will ever have, and have stood the test gloriously and triumphantly. There is no danger of their revolt, under any circumstances. Not only can God trust them; but other angels can trust them, and we can trust them. This is a great and unmistakable good, both to them and to all who have any occasion for their services.

The same thing has taken place and become known in regard to those who fell.

Their character is also fixed, and published to all who have need to be warned against them. They chose to rebel against God under the strongest influences possible to deter and prevent their apostacy. That choice was deliberate. It will never be changed. No influence stronger than those they have already spurned and defied can be brought to bear upon them. No new light of truth with which they were unacquainted can ever fall upon their minds or hearts. They are lost; "kept in everlasting bonds" of stubborn resistance to the will of God, "under darkness, unto the judgment of the great day."

I quoted above Peter's warning; let me add mine. No poor, inconsiderate mortal can possibly be guilty of greater folly than when he thinks light of the infernal influences to which he is constantly exposed, and against which he should be constantly watchful and in firmest attitude of resistance.

"Satan with malicious art,
    Watches each unguarded heart."

Demons, who were endowed at the commencement of their existence with angelic capacities for knowledge, growth, and influence over others, and who have had almost six thousand years of successful experience in leading unsuspecting, and even watchful, souls into sin, must have become very artful and skillful in their diabolical work, ere this time. Let us then be on our guard against all those influences, "whose coming is according to the workings of Satan, with all power and signs and lying wonders, and with all deceit of unrighteousness for them that perish; because they received not the love of the truth, that they might be saved." "Resist the devil, and he will flee from you."

(4) One of the most sensible of the questions asked on this subject, and one of the easiest to answer, in the light of the nature of moral agency, is, Why were the fallen angels cast down to the earth, to tempt the new, innocent, ignorant, unsuspecting race of man? Can any good be traced to this act? This is a question to which every one, young and old, should have a ready answer. The following is my way of pre-

senting it. It was that they might accomplish in man just what they had already accomplished among the angels. It was as necessary, as important, that men should be tried, that they should have established characters, that their loyalty to God and to the welfare of the race to which they belonged, or their disloyalty, should be manifested, as it was that these facts and dispositions in the angels should be manifested. Men were created for trusts, for labors, for influences, for responsibilities, as great, as important, as were the angels, perhaps even greater. This is a fact that most of the race, up to this time, seem to have never thought of, much less to have seriously comprehended. It is as important to know whom to trust, and whom not to trust, among men as among angels. God knew all this, and chose this manner of testing the loyalty, and showing the disloyalty, of each individual of our race; at least of each and every one who attains the estate of accountability.

Doubtless this was the wisest and best method that could be devised for this purpose; else he who is infinite in wisdom and goodness would not have chosen it. This is a point that should be always assumed, God has made no mistakes. Moreover, it makes no difference to us. If the testing had not been done in this way, it would have been done in some other way, equally unwelcome, probably more disagreeable and objectionable. Let us be content.

LECTURE IX.

THE GODHEAD.

It has been said that "The proper study of mankind is man." That is true, but it is only a part of the truth. While man furnishes an interesting and profitable study for the scientist, the humanitarian, the moralist and the historian, the careful study of God is still more important and profitable. Let us not shrink now from a free, unrestrained, unrestricted approach to this study, because God is Infinite and we are finite; nor because God is Holy and we are sinful. The more we know about God, the better for us. Many are so filled with awe and reverence at the very thought of God, that they exclaim with ignorant and unwise Zophar, "Canst thou by searching find out God?" and, resting there, remain in ignorance.

Whatever there may be about the Uncaused Cause of all things that is "past finding out," there is much respecting him that may be known as clearly and as positively as respecting ourselves; and what we may know of him is, if possible, of more interest and of more importance to us than what we know of ourselves. Bear in mind, also, that, though the prophet said, "Verily thou art a God that hideth thyself," yet God shrinks from no investigation. He is not only willing but anxious that we should know all about him that we can find out, by most diligent inquiry, closest observation, most profound investigation, and greatest intimacy. While vain and idle speculation, guesses, and unfounded assumptions should not be indulged in nor encouraged in any line of inquiry, there is not a fact hidden, neither in his works, nor in his essence, nor in his mode of existence, nor in his methods of manifestation or operation, that God holds too sacred for our inquiry. We shall approach this subject, then, with the same fearless freedom with which we would inquire whether the sun is the center of our solar system.

The word "Godhead," as used in Col. ii. 9, "In him dwelleth all the fullness of the Godhead;" is itself suggestive of a plurality of persons. If no other idea than that of unity had ever been entertained, as pertaining to the Deity, it is reasonable to suppose that but one name would have been given him, and that name would not have been Godhead.

The plurality of persons in the Godhead is also clearly intimated in the name by which the Creator was first designated. That name, in the Hebrew language, is ELOHIM, and is in the plural number. It is found in the first verse of the book of Genesis, and is used as the name of God 2222 times in the Old Testament. In Gen. i. 26, we read, "Let us make man in our image, after our likeness." These phrases, "our image, our likeness," I understand to refer to their individual moral agency, for this is the point of "likeness" between God and man, by which the fact of plurality is made still more emphatic. It is not the image of the One Infinite and Eternal, nor of the two conceived of as a unit, but of each individually. One other passage, Gen. iii. 22, "The man is become as one of us," is regarded by many commentators as even stronger evidence than the foregoing of plurality in the Godhead. Those who wish to avoid this conclusion insist that this is the *pluralis excellentiæ*, as rulers (and many others) use the plural pronoun we, instead of the singular I; but I think it is the *pluralis personarum*, the plural being used because it represents a plurality of persons.

Of the persons comprehended in the Godhead, the self-existent Originator of all things (except himself) must be one; and, of course, the First. If the universe, either of matter or of spirit, shows evidences of design, he must be the Designer; if evidences of a plan, he is the Planner; if there is a display of wisdom and power, these must be attributes that are inherent in his nature. Thus we conclude, without the possibility of error, that the First Person in the Godhead is the Eternal, Infinite, Omniscient, Omnipotent Deity—the Uncaused Cause of all things; who is, in the English language, called God.

We are now prepared to make some

inquiries respecting this First Person in the Godhead.

Under this head, it is not our purpose to adduce evidences of the existence of God, but to notice certain facts concerning his attributes that seem obscure to some, and whose nature does not generally seem to be clearly understood.

The attributes of God are of two kinds; Necessary and Moral.

God's Necessary Attributes are those that belong to him of necessity, as contrasted with those that are his from choice. They exist in his constitution. It is no irreverence to say that God could not divest himself of one of these attributes, if he wished to do so. I call these Necessary Attributes, instead of "Natural Attributes," because Moral Attributes are just as consistent with God's nature, just as natural to his constitution, as these are. Hence natural and moral are not terms of contrast, while necessary and moral are distinctively antithetic.

God's Moral Attributes are qualities of character. They belong to God as the result of the choices he makes. I do not mean that God makes any attribute the object of his choice. These attributes belong to him because of the things he voluntarily chooses to do—the courses of conduct he chooses to pursue—in his relations with other intelligences. If he were the only intelligence in the universe, his Necessary Attributes would still belong to him; but a moral attribute would be impossible, except as it might exist as a state of mind, a voluntary disposition to do certain things, if there were an occasion.

I am anxious all should get a clear and correct notion on these points. It is for lack of clear ideas of the nature and condition and results of moral action, moral agency, that so many strange theological notions are held, that people believe only because they have been told that they are taught in the Bible. Such persons often say, "I believe that doctrine, not because I apprehend it as a truth, but because it is taught in our pulpits, and people say it is taught in the Bible." Now I want to say distinctly, I hold no such doctrines, more properly called "dogmas." I believe I have a reason for every doctrine I hold, and I will never ask any man to believe a doctrine, nor perform an act as a duty, for which I cannot give him a reason, and a reason whose reasonableness he can apprehend and comprehend.

I. What are the Necessary Attributes of God?

1. *Personality*. This attribute belongs necessarily to every self-determining intelligence. God is such an intelligence, hence a person. Self-consciousness is the determining fact of personality. Any being who is conscious of selfhood; any being who realizes I am, I think, I feel, I will, is a person. This self-consciousness belongs to God, not from choice but of necessity, hence personality is one of his Necessary Attributes.

2. *Eternity*. This means having neither beginning nor end. This is a necessary affirmation of the reason. That he had no beginning is certain, because there was no intelligent existence before him to give him being; hence he must of necessity be the Uncaused Cause.

3. *Omnipotence.* This is power to accomplish whatever is an object of power. It does not apply to any thing to which power cannot be applied. It is power unlimited by any other power. The fact that God is Omnipotent is ground for asserting that he can do any thing that requires power for its performance; but it is ground for nothing else. If he can do other things, it is not because he is Omnipotent. His ability to think, to feel, to will, is not based upon his Omnipotence. Moreover, there are many things he cannot do at all. For instance, God cannot find a shorter distance between two points than a straight line. That is a fact he did not create, and that he cannot change. Neither can he coerce the will of any being to whom he has given the power of choice. The will of every moral agent in the universe is sovereign, self-determining; just as independent of the will of God, in its action, as the will of God is independent of my will or yours. The Omnipotence of God was of no avail in devising or executing the plan of salvation. God cannot save sinners from their

sins by his own Omnipotence. If he were to prevent them, by physical force, from executing their wicked purposes, he could not coerce their intention, and the sin lies in the intention, not in the execution of the intention. Such hindrance would not prevent the sin. "He that hateth his brother is a murderer," though circumstances may restrain him from taking his brother's life.

4. *Omniscience.* The meaning of this attribute is that all things knowable are known to God. No one doubts that God knows every thing that has transpired in the past, and every thing that is now transpiring. Does he know the future? Assuredly; all that ever will transpire, through the ages of eternity. Nor is this all. Not only are the past, the present and the future known to him. Every thing that would have been, had a different choice been made by each intelligence in the universe, at each alternative point, and every thing that might be but will not be, are just as clearly known to him as the past and the present. Omniscience comprehends not only facts that have been or will be, but all possibilities as well, inclu-

ding the whole line of events that would follow each of these possible choices, down into the eternal ages. You exclaim "Incomprehensible!" Yes, such knowledge is incomprehensible; but that it is and must be so is not incomprehensible.

It was said of a celebrated chess-player that he knew not only what would be the effect upon the whole future of the game, of each move made upon the chess-board; but the possible effect of each move that could be made, from the commencement to the end of the game. If a human mind can comprehend not only the actualities but the possibilities of a game of chess, why should the statement that the infinite mind comprehends all the possibilities of the universe stagger any one?

Do not say, "I cannot understand it." Turn on the light and look. See and understand all you can; and from what you do see, judge of that which may be beyond your sight. From a few observations, the astromomer calculates the entire orbit of a distant planet, of which he had no previous knowledge; so from his works, and from his word, and from his dealings with our own hearts, we may learn a great deal about God.

One practical thought, of great significance and great encouragement, comes to my mind right here. All thoughts, as well as deeds, are known to the infinite mind; but the knowledge of finite minds, even of the angels, both good and bad, is confined to manifestations of thoughts. They cannot know our thoughts as God knows them. Even the devil does not know what we think, unless our thought is revealed by some form of expression.

5. *Omnipresence* is another Necessary Attribute of God. This does not mean that God is infinitely large. "His center is everywhere, and his circumference nowhere," though the prevailing idea of his Omnipresence cannot be true. "His presence fills immensity" is more nearly correct, provided you make a clear discrimination between his presence and the magnitude of his person.

In order to a proper understanding of this attribute, it is necessary to remove a very common, and almost universal, misconception of the divine mode of existence. I dislike exceedingly the apparent arrogance and self-conceit with which I am liable to be charged, for presuming to present as truth theories and ideas that differ from those held and taught by far more learned and profound thinkers than myself, and made sacred by the faith of ages, until men have almost ceased to inquire into the foundation on which they rest. I have no ambition to be an iconoclast, nor do I lack regard for the opinions of others, nor reverence for the great and scholarly men of the past; but he is not worthy to be a teacher who has not "the courage of his own convictions," which is but another expression for daring to differ from others. Luther said, "Popes have erred and so have councils;" and probably the great men of the past, as well as those of the present, have erred; and smaller men who come after them may detect and correct their errors.

The error to which I refer is the doctrine that God is an unsubstantial though intelligent force, energy, an abstraction, an idea, a conception, a myth, a name, an incomprehensible imagination, "without body or parts," and in no sense a substance, an entity, having form and occupying a particular locality in space. As soon as one suggests the idea of a substantial essence, men are shocked, and cry out "Materialism! Materialism!" This is only the cry of "mad dog." Substantialism is no more materialism than spiritism is materialism. Angels are spirits, and saints are spirits; does anyone doubt that they are substantial existences? or suppose that their bodily forms are composed of matter? So is God a Spirit.

An intelligent being, whatever its mode of existence, must think, feel and will. Now, a force, an energy, a myth, a conception, an imagination, cannot think. A thought cannot think; a feeling cannot feel; a volition cannot will. Where there is thought, there is something that thinks; and so of feeling and of willing. Passages of Scripture are numerous in which different organs of the body are attributed to God. These are usually explained as figurative; language used only by way of accommodation, that it may be more intelligible to us. Yet writers often speak of the "Divine substance," the "Divine essence."

Now, be assured, where there is substance, however ethereal, however refined, however divine, it has form and occupies space, and a limited amount of space at that. That being which has no substance, no form, no location, is only an imaginary being—only a myth, a thought, an imagination, an abstraction. Such a being never planned this universe. An unsubstantial intelligent person is impossible, unthinkable.

If you ask me, Where is God located? where is the throne on which he sits as a Sovereign? where he hold his court, surrounded by the angels that always behold his face? my answer is, I do not know. There must be a center of the universe somewhere; it may be there.

This question must be considered from our standpoint, not from his. He is not Omnipresent in the sense that he is everywhere bodily; but because everything is in his presence. Nothing can be hidden from him. A teacher sits upon the rostrum in a school-room, and every thing in the room is in his presence. Now, if the teacher could read the thoughts, intentions and motives of each pupil, and knew, without effort, everything that transpired in the room, we would have a miniature representation of the Omnipresence of God in the universe. The teacher does not fill the school-room, but everything in the school-room is in his presence. So God does not fill infinite space, but everything in space is in his presence. Does not this presentation of the subject coincide with the presentations found in the word of God? Read Isa. vi. 1. "I saw the Lord sitting upon a throne, high and lifted up." Read also Dan. vii. 9, 10, and Rev. iv. 2–6. Ps. ciii. 19, "Jehovah hath established his throne in the heavens;" and cxxxix. 7–12, "Whither shall I go from thy Spirit? or whither shall I flee from thy presence? if I ascend into heaven, thou art there; if I make my bed in Sheol, behold thou art there. If I take the wings of the morning, and dwell in the uppermost parts of the sea, even there shall thy hand lead me, and thy right hand shall hold me. If I say, Surely the darkness shall overwhelm me, and the light about me shall be night, even the darkness hideth not from thee, but the night shineth as the day. The darkness and the light are both alike to thee." Luke i. 19. "The angel answering said unto him, I am Gabriel, that stand in the presence of God." Passages that speak of God's presence, his face, eyes, ears, hands, feet, and other parts of his body, are numerous. Undoubtedly this language is employed to give us a clear and truthful conception of God; and what can be more helpful to that end than the statement of facts as they are? I do not believe that the Scriptures are full of fables and false statements, in order to convey truths of the greatest importance to human minds. I know of no better way to teach truth to others than to tell them the truth as it is. When Scripture language is figurative or poetical, there will always be some attendant fact or circumstance that will suggest that fact.

II. The Moral Attributes of God.

My object, under this head, is not to enumerate all the Moral Attributes of the

Deity, but to mention such of them as are necessary to show their nature, and to demonstrate the fact that God must be a moral agent. Moral attributes are qualities of moral character, and can belong only to a moral agent. The fact that God possesses these attributes, a fact that is undisputed, is positive evidence that he is a moral agent.

Whatever God is morally, he is from choice, and that choice must be made in the presence of an alternative. Right here, at the very threshhold of our inquiry, lies an immense stumblingblock. Men have so long considered it unpardonable irreverence to reason respecting God, as they would reason in other things, that they are shocked at the very suggestion that God's attributes are not all inherent qualities, or facts, of his constitution, belonging to him of necessity. They suppose that God is holy and good, just and merciful, for the same reason that he is eternal and omniscient; because it is a necessity of his being, and he could not, under any possibility, be otherwise. This error must be abandoned, or no adequate idea of God can be entertained. The fact that "we praise God for his goodness," implies that we regard it as a virtue in him to be good, and must be accepted as evidence that he is good from choice and not from necessity; and this is moral agency.

But we are asked, "Does not moral agency necessitate the possibility of sinning? Do you think that God can sin? Do not the Scriptures say that God cannot lie?" In answer to these questions, let me ask some questions. Suppose the beautiful story of Washington, the hatchet and the cherry tree, to be true; and that the little boy Washington did say, "Father you know I cannot tell a lie;" do you understand that the lad had no power to tell a lie, that it was an impossibility of his constitution? or that he did not choose to tell a lie? that it was a moral, not a physical, impossibility? Who would say the boy could not have told a lie, had he chosen to do so?

Again, there sits before me a mother. In her arms rests a sleeping infant. I place a glittering dagger in her hand, and bid her thrust it through the heart of that infant. In an instant, she flings the dagger to the floor, and with an expression of horror upon her countenance she exclaims, "I cannot kill my babe." Would anyone suppose she meant that she had not the physical strength to do it? Thus the fact that God is good, that he cannot lie, rests in his choice, in the moral integrity and purpose of his will, not in any inability. Does anyone suppose that God has endowed mortals with abilities that he does not possess himself? Were that the case man would not have been created in the image of God.

Since, then, every virtue, every trait of moral character, is a moral attribute, and since God possesses them all, his moral attributes are very numerous. Mr. Finney enumerates thirty-seven of them; and includes them all in the one all-embracing attribute Love. This conception of all moral attributes is undoubtedly correct. We shall follow it, mentioning, however, only a few of the leading attributes, and showing that they all center in love, and never conflict or clash one with another.

1. God is Love. As an attribute of God, what is Love?

(1) It is not parental love. Parental love is an instinct. It is found in brutes as well as in human beings. It is a virtue only in so far as it is acquiesced in voluntarily, in the presence of the alternative of rejecting it. While it is not a positive virtue in the human mother to love her offspring, it would be a positive sin in her not to love it; for that would require a positive purpose. No mother could hate her offspring instinctively. It may be said that all the instincts of a parent belong to our heavenly Father; but it is not because of these that we affirm that "God is Love." He claims no virtue for this.

(2) It is not friendship, however strong. The strongest friendship between individuals may be perfectly consistent with pure selfishness towards all others, and may arise from a selfish motive between themselves.

(3.) It is not the love of one sex for the other. That is also instinctive; and its exercise may be right or wrong according to circumstances.

(4) It is the voluntary exercise of good-willing, *bene volens*, benevolence. God wills the good, the highest good, of every sentient creature. This love has no respect whatever to the moral character of the person loved. He wishes the sinner well as well as the saint. "He maketh his sun to rise on the evil and the good, and sendeth rain on the just and the unjust." "God so loved the world that he gave his only begotten Son." This is also the love he requires, when he says, "Love your enemies and pray for them that persecute you;" also, "Thou shalt love thy neighbor as thyself." Many, misinterpreting this command, supposing it to mean that they must feel the same affectionate attachment to their disobliging, morose, hateful, hostile, neighbor, as they feel for the members of their own families and their most intimate and accommodating friends, rebel against the precept, and declare that obedience to it is impossible; while many others, intent on doing all the Savior requires of them, strive to realize such affection for their bitterest enemies; and reproach themselves for lack of grace

and faith, because their efforts are futile. Let me assure all such that no such love is required or commanded. The language of the precept will bear no such intrepretation. It does not read thou shalt love thy neighbor as thou lovest thy wife, thy husband, thy child, thy friend. Your love for yourself is the standard, and what is that love? Is it affection? Never!

Did you ever feel prompted to throw your loving arms around the reflection of your own person in a mirror? or to imprint a kiss upon the reflection of your own fair cheek? Never! What then? The dearest thing to every man, except his life, is his rights. Benevolence requires of every one that he regard the rights and the welfare of his neighbor, even his enemy, as carefully, as truly, as sacredly, as he regards his own rights and welfare. They who rejoice when their enemy stumbleth, and are glad when calamities overtake him, disobey this precept; but those who wish even their enemies well, even though they do not love them, and delight in their companionship, as they do their own families, obey it. In the light of this illustration and explanation, we may discover and comprehend what Love is as an attribute of God. These two kinds of love have been known among theologians as Love of Benevolence, and Love of Complacency.

2. At the head of all attributes of Love stands Justice. "The Lord is our Judge; the Lord is our Lawgiver; the Lord is our King." The first necessity in him who sustains these relations to intelligent beings is the disposition to treat each one according to his intrinsic merit or desert. To this attribute we give the name Justice. As related to crime, it considers the well-being not of the criminal alone, but of the entire community, including the lawgiver himself; and deals with the offender as the good of all concerned demands.

This attribute is often misunderstood. Many suppose its intent, its object, is to inflict deserved punishment for misconduct; that is, visit upon the offender an amount of suffering that Justice will take as an equivalent or satisfaction for the offence. This is a great mistake. There is no such function in the government of God. He has no attribute whose intent is punitive. I grant that the word punish and its derivatives are found many times in the Scriptures. So are the words wrath, anger, vengeance, as applied to God; but none of these words are to be understood as referring to the motive by which God is actuated in visiting its just deserts upon sin. They represent the view men take of the act of punishment, while they (the men) are ignorant or unobservant of the motive that prompts the act. The same is true, theoretically at least, in human governments. Men are fined, or sent to prison, not for the purpose of wreaking vengeance upon them, but with the hope that they may be reformed thereby; and when light punishment fails in effecting this result, and the offender becomes incorrigible, and is imprisoned for life, or put to death, the intent of the government is not vengeance but the protection of community, and as a warning to others of the consequences of transgression. This is, at least, the divine intent in authorizing human governments, whether it is so understood by men or not. Possibly, there may be much yet to learn on this point.

Let the fact be deeply impressed upon every mind, that Love is the underlying principle of all the offices and functions of Justice; not only toward the well-deserving, in suitably rewarding meritorious conduct; but toward the ill-deserving, in meting out suitable punishments. The object, in the latter case, being corrective, first of the offender himself, and secondly of the disposition of others to commit the same crime; and also the safety and welfare of community. "When the scorner is punished, the simple is made wise."

3. Mercy. This is also an attribute of Love. As representative of an attitude of the divine will, Mercy is a disposition to pardon the guilty. In the exercise of this disposition, the welfare of community must be carefully guarded. (This point is treated in Lecture vi. 7). Hence mercy can be shown only when Justice, as guardian of the rights and welfare of the whole, is satisfied, and consents that the offender may be pardoned; and Justice can be executed only

when Mercy, all her merciful offices spurned, retires from her efforts, and abandons the sinner to his fate. This spurning of Mercy is the sin against the Holy Spirit, that hath never forgiveness, neither in this world nor in the world to come.

Though the moral attributes of God are numerous, none could better illustrate and enforce the doctrine of his moral agency than those that have already been mentioned. If God is Love, benevolence itself, regarding alike the well-being of enemies and friends, of those who are in rebellion against, and of those who are loyal to, his government, it must surely be evident to all that it is because he chooses that attitude towards them, not because it is an unalterable necessity of his constitution. The same is also true in regard to all his Moral Attributes.

4. One thought more is worthy of our notice under this head. In the Scriptures men are often called upon to thank and praise the Lord. For what do they praise him? Invariably for things that he does voluntarily. Note the following as examples: Ps. cvii. 1, "O give thanks unto Jehovah;

for he is good; for his loving kindness endureth forever." Four times, also, in the same psalm, "O that men would praise Jehovah for his loving kindness, and for his wonderful works to the children of men!" Ps. cxxxvi. commences "O give thanks unto Jehovah, for he is good; for his loving kindness endureth forever;" and every one of the twenty-six verses of this psalm mentions some voluntary act of his for which thanks should be given him. We may reverence and adore God for what he is inherently, constitutionally—for his Omnipotence, Omniscience, etc.—but we can praise him only for what he does, and for what he is by virtue of his voluntary state of mind. Hence God is a Moral Agent.

THE EXECUTIVE DEITY—THE WORD—THE SON

Associated with the One Infinite and Eternal God is another distinct and individual personage. This second person in the Godhead is the first thing in the universe that ever had existence separate from the Infinite and Eternal ONE. He is designated in the Scriptures by a very large number of distinctive and significant appellations, and is the Executive Diety, through whom all the works of God have been and will be performed.

He is the Word that formulated and gave expression to the creative fiat; the Jehovah Elohim who talked with Adam in the garden of Eden; the Jehovah who talked with Noah, Abraham, Moses, with the High Priest from between the cherubim, and with the prophets at a later day. He was the "Angel of the Covenant," the "Captain of the Lord's Host." It was his finger that wrote the commandments upon the tables of stone, and his voice that caused the earth to quake and the people to tremble. In the fullness of time he made his appearance on earth as the babe of Bethlehem—the Son of God and the son of man. All this and much more will be clearly shown as we proceed.

1. Gen. i. 1, "In the beginning, God." John i. 1, "In the beginning was the Word." These phases refer, without doubt, to the initial moment of divine activity, when the stagnation of eternity was broken by an

event. ELOHIM existed then; the Infinite and Eternal ONE, and the WORD: the Father and the Son. Hence it appears that "The Word" was the first name by which the Son of God was known. Now a word is an idea expressed. It is the thing, the sound, the vocable, that expresses, gives form to, in a certain sense materializes and renders perceptible to one intelligence the idea, the thought, of another. This Word was the first expression, manifestation, ever given to a thought, an idea, a plan, a purpose, of the Infinite and Eternal God. He was in the beginning, at the beginning, and the beginning itself.

2. "The Word was with God" (John i. 1). This is a remarkable statement. It can not be made intelligibly of a simple sound of the voice, a vocable. You cannot say a spoken word is with him who uttered it. It must mean more than that. What does it mean? It means that "The Word" is the distinctive and distinguishing appellation of a separate individual, a second person in the Godhead. He is an invisible idea, thought, purpose, represented in a sub-

stantial form, endowed with life, intelligence, personality. Having dwelt during the preceding eternity as a concept in the mind of the Father, he is now a distinct, self-acting, self-conscious, responsible individuality; his appellation—the Word—indicating both his origin and his character.

On this important point let us take his own testimony, when he was on earth as the Son of God and the son of man. John viii. 42, "I came forth and am come from God; neither have I come of myself, but he sent me." John xvi. 28, "I came out from the Father, and am come into the world; again I leave the world, and go unto the Father." John vi. 38, "I am come down from heaven not to do my own will, but the will of him who sent me." Two wills can exist only where there are two personalities.

If a person who leaves another and returns to him again, is not a separate and distinct individual from the one whom he leaves and to whom he returns; and if the one who is sent is not a separate individual from him who sends, tell me, ye who can, how one individual may be distinguished from another, so that we shall know there are two instead of one.

How far back we must turn the dial in order to find the beginning of his independent personality, we may judge from such passages as the following: Col. i. 17, 15. "He is before all things," "The image of the invisible God, the first-born of all creation." Rev. iii. 14, "The beginning of the creation of God;" not the first thing created, but the agent through which the whole creation, from the beginning, was effected John i. 3, "All things were made through him; and without him was not anything made." John xvii, 5, "O Father glorify thou me with thine own self with the glory which I had with thee before the world was."

3. "The word was God" (John i, 1). This declaration respecting the word has been greatly misunderstood. Many have supposed it was the intention of John, and of the inspiring Spirit, to affirm that he was personally and individually identical with the Father in whom and from whom he had his origin, and with whom he was. With one breath such exegetes predicate of each a

personal, individual identity; with the next they deny their dualty, and declare the two to be one personal identity. When asked to explain the contradiction, their answer is, "It is a mystery, beyond human comprehension. No one attempts to explain it. It must, however, be true; for it is the plain declaration of the inspired word. God has said it, and I must believe it. I believe what the Scriptures say, whether it accords with or contradicts my reason. When God speaks, no one should presume to reason."

Before considering the meaning of the text, I must be permitted a brief digression, in order to say a few words respecting this attitude of mind. As I apprehend it, this is a false conception of faith. He who says he believes a statement that contradicts his own positive knowledge of facts, let the statement come from whatever source it may, stultifies his reason, falsifies his convictions, and degrades his manhood. Such a thing can not be done. It is not in the power of a rational being. We may believe, and must believe, multitudes of facts whose causes and sources are beyond our rational comprehension; but to believe that which contradicts reason is impossible. It is not difficult to believe that two, three, or any number of separate entities, existences, whether material or spiritual, may be of like essence, substance, or material; nor that two, three, or any number of individual personalities, each an independent, self-conscious *ego*, may exist and act in perfect harmony of purpose, thought and feeling, in perfect coincidence of judgment and unity of action; but the affirmation that two separate units, whether of matter, of essence, of substance, of spirit, of self-conscious personality, or of whatever else may be supposable, however homogeneous in substance or harmonious in thought and volition, may be one unit of the same kind, can not be believed by any intelligent, reasoning being in the universe. Nor does this fact in any degree compromise the declarations of the word of God, or weaken the most profound faith in that word. The most contradictory statements that can be found in the Bible, respecting the Supreme Father and the submissive and obedient Son, are perfectly harmonious, when correctly interpreted. "I and my Father are one," "My Father is greater than I," "No man hath seen God at any time;" "He that hath seen me hath seen the Father," are perfectly harmonious and consistent one with another, and each with all the rest, when truthfully interpreted. There is not even the semblance of a contradiction or discrepancy.

In order to a clear, positive, reliable understanding of the proposition, "The Word was God," reference must be had to the Greek, the language in which this gospel was written. Even from an accurate English translation, its true meaning is not so much as suggested; while from the Greek it is clearly demonstrable. The Greek reads, Theos (God) en (was) ho (the) logos (word). Why not translate this, God was the Word, placing each word in the order in which it is found in the original? Because such a translation would violate a very important rule of the Greek language. That rule is, "In a simple proposition, the subject usually takes the article and the predicate does not." No one will dispute that this is a plain example under that rule. Logos, then, having the article, is the subject of the proposition; and Theos, not having the article, is the predicate. Hence we translate, The Word was God.

Does this mean that the personal Word was the personal God? To this inquiry we invite the most careful and candid attention, particularly of Greek scholars, hoping at the same time, to make our exposition intelligible to all. If the Greek read, ho theos en ho logos, the God was the Word, either God or Word might be the subject, and the other the predicate. It would then mean, The personal Word was the personal God; or the personal God was the personal Word: the two terms of the proposition being identical, either may be properly considered as subject, and the other as predicate. Manifestly, then, if John had intended to make that statement, he would have used that form. Conversely, since he did not use that form, he did not intend to make that statement. What then did John mean to state? He meant to state that the Word—the living personal Word—was of the same essence, substance, nature as the Supreme and Infinite God, his Father. The Word was Divine. He inherited (speaking after the manner of men) the intellectual endowments of the Father, as well as homogeneity of essence and substance with him; on account of which he possessed constitutionally the natural endowments that qualified him for and enabled him to perform the great works assigned to him to do.

His faithful performance of these works, as well as the moral attributes of his character, were all dependent upon his choices, the same as in the case of any other moral agent, his Father for instance; but note well, none of the Necessary Attributes (see page 182), that exist in infinite degree as inseparable characteristics of the Supreme One, belong essentially, inherently, to him. He is neither Eternal, Omniscient nor Omnipotent. In his own nature and constitution he is not Infinite. Do not be shocked at this. If what has already been shown, page 117, respecting the separate individuality of the Word, supported by quotations from the Savior's own lips, may be relied upon, this proposition is self-evident. Nothing that is Infinite can be dual or plural. The oneness of Infinity is as self-evident as the axioms of mathematics. Infinity necessitates unity. One infinite space fills immensity; no room can be found for another. One infinite duration comprehends eternity; no other eternity can either precede or follow it. One infinite intelligence embraces all mental capacities and powers; there can be neither occasion for nor possibility of another.

4. His qualifications.

In the performance of the works committed to him as the Executive Deity, whatever of wisdom and power was necessary, beyond what was attainable in his own developement, was furnished without stint or limit by the Father, who was ever present with him, and all of whose infinite resources were at his command. Col. i. 19, "It was the good pleasure of the Father that in him should all the fullness dwell." Col. ii. 9, "In him dwelleth all the fullness of the Godhead." Thus nothing could be lacking in him that it was in the power of the

Father to supply. Jesus' own words in this matter fully explain the situation. John iii. 34, "He whom God hath sent speaketh the words of God; for he giveth not the Spirit by measure." John, v. 20, "The Father loveth the Son and showeth him all things that himself doeth." Mat xi. 27, "All things have been delivered unto me of my Father." Mat. xxviii. 18, "All authority hath been given unto me in heaven and on earth." John viii. 28, 29, 42, "I do nothing of myself; but as the Father taught me, I speak these things. And he that sent me is with me; he hath not left me alone, for I do always the things that are pleasing to him. I came forth and am come from God; neither have I come of myself, but he sent me." John xii. 49, "I spake not from myself; but the Father who sent me, he hath given me a commandment, what I should say and what I should speak. The things, therefore, which I speak, even as the Father hath said unto me, so I speak." John xiv. 10, "The words that I say unto you I speak not from myself; but the Father abiding in me doeth his works." Many other passages might be quoted to the same end; but it must be manifest to every candid reader that it is utterly impossible that the Infinite One should use such language respecting himself. Such language is possible only for one who is conscious both of the high exaltation of the position he occupies in the universe, of the fullness of his qualifications to meet his responsibilities, and of his complete dependence upon a superior, to whom he delights to attribute all the authority under which he acts, and all the wisdom and power that are manifest in and through him. The subterfuge to which many resort, that Jesus spoke sometimes as a man and at others as God, only involves those who resort to it in still more inextricable difficulties and inconsistencies. We believe the view here presented is fully consistent with the Scriptures, with reason, and with common sense; while the views that have been commonly held in the past are arbitrary, and inconsistent with all of these. In the Son of God, as here presented, we have a personage, who fully answers to the description that is found in Heb. i. 3, "Who being the effulgence (*apaugasma*, reflected splendor) of his glory, and the very image (*charakter*, stamp, impress, exact likeness) of his substance (*hupostaceos*, substance, essence, being)." Hence he is unquestionably and indisputably Divine; and at this initial period of his existence only Divine—the Executive Deity.

5. Should divine worship be rendered to the Son of God? This is a question of very great importance, since the object one worships determines whether he is a servant of the true God or a heathen.

What we call worship has its origin in the constitutional endowment of our nature, that prompts admiration and deferential deportment towards another, whom we suppose to be superior in some respect, to ourselves. Its elements are admiration, praise, petition and thanksgiving. Admiration is suggested by the superiority recognized. When exercised towards the Supreme Being, and prompted by love and devotion in the highest degree, we call it adoration. This is the strongest word in our language with which to express loving, filial, supreme honor, loyalty, devotion.

Praise is properly rendered only for the virtues of moral character. We "praise God for his loving-kindness, and for his wonderful works to the children of men." These are acts that indicate praiseworthy qualities of character. They are the products of volition, not inherent and necessary attributes. We adore God for his moral attributes; but also and more especially for his necessary attributes—Eternity, Infinity, Omniscience, Omnipresence, Omnipotence. For these latter, however we cannot praise him; because they belong to him from necessity and not from choice.

We offer petition to God for the things that we need and have not. In doing this, we recognize him as having in his possession and at his disposal all the resources of the universe; also his promises, "Ask and ye shall receive;" "No good thing will he withhold from them that walk uprightly."

Thanksgiving, as an act of divine worship, is an expression of gratitude to God for what he is and for what he does. It must be borne in mind, however, that thanksgiving, like praise, belongs to God only for what he is from choice, not from necessity. We may thank God because he is Love; but we cannot thank him because he is Infinite and Eternal. This analysis should impress us with the fact that worship must be intelligent as well as emotional, in order to be acceptable to God and profitable to the worshiper.

Doubtless it will occur to the reader that there is much included in these acts, considered severally, that pertains to our fellow men as well as to God; that the difference between adoration and admiration is only a difference in degree, not in kind; and that praise, petition and thanksgiving are as appropriate when given to a deserving fellow mortal, as when rendered to God. All these facts have much to do with the question of worshiping our Lord Jesus Christ, to which we will now come directly.

We have already shown that all the fullness of the Godhead dwells in him; that all the infinite attributes of the Supreme One are practically, though not in an absolute sense, his; that he is the Executive Deity, in creation, redemption and judgment; that he is the Jehovah of the old dispensation, and the Immanuel (God with us) of the new; and that he is essentially and substantially divine in his constitution and nature. Add to all this the wonderful, the astonishing fact that "He loved us, and gave himself for us," that "while we were yet sinners, Christ died for us," and do we not find in him everything required to challenge and warrant not admiration only but adoration? Is he not also worthy of the highest praise and thanksgiving we are capable of rendering? Is it not of him we are to obtain pardon of sin and eternal life? I John v. 11, "God gave unto us eternal life, and this life is in his Son;" Mat. xi. 28, "Come unto me all ye that labor and are heavy-laden, and I will give you rest." Are not the resources of the universe, "all power in heaven and in earth," in his hand, and at his disposal, and should we not go to him with our petitions, whatever we may want or desire? Thus all the elements of worship, divine worship, are due to him, if not in the very highest degree, at least in a degree so high, so broad, so great, that to discriminate between him and any other, even the Father Almighty, would be difficult if not practically impossible. Who, while gazing into the heavens, can discover that one of the heavenly bodies is nearer his eye than another? and yet their distances differ by millions of miles. The moon seems to the naked eye to lie in the same field with the most distant star. Thus it is with the Son of God, as related to us and to the Infinite Father. Though the Father is infinite and the Son finite, to our view and for all practical purposes both are in the same heavenly plane. So far as we, our wants and necessities, are concerned, the Son is equal to the Father. His authority, his powers, his official capabilities, are the same; and the same worship is due him. He is "God Almighty," or, as Adam Clarke says, commenting on Ex. vi. 3, "God All-sufficient;" and is so called in many places in the Scriptures.

Conceding, though scarcely from conviction of its truth, that the Magi (Mat. ii, 1) had no idea of divine honor to the infant

Jesus, when they "fell down and worshipped him," such a fact can not be conceded in such cases as the following: Matt. viii, 2, "There came to him a leper and worshipped him, saying, Lord, if thou wilt, thou canst make me clean." The act of worship, in this case, consisted in addressing Jesus as "Lord," ascribing to him supernatural power, and reverentially beseeching him to perform a miraculous act of healing. This is quite above the homage rendered to kings, and is clearly a recognition, on the part of the suppliant, of the divine nature and power of the Savior. A still more positive instance, one whose import and intent can not be reasonably questioned, is recorded in Matt. xiv, 33, "They that were in the boat worshipped him, saying, Of a truth thou art the Son of God." Jesus had walked from the shore upon the water, in a fearful storm, to rescue his imperiled disciples. Peter, at his command, had stepped boldly out of the boat upon the water to meet him; but, losing faith, had been saved from drowning by the outstretched hand of the Master. They entered the boat safely, and the wind ceased. At this juncture, the disciples "worshipped him." Can this worship mean anything less than recognizing in him divine power? ascribing to him divine honor? and rendering to him praise and thanksgiving as unto their Sovereign King and Lord? Again, on the morning of the resurrection, when the two Marys (Mat. xxviii, 8, 9) "ran to bring the disciples word, and "Jesus met them, saying, All hail! And they came and took hold of his feet, and worshipped him." If this does not mean divine worship, would it not be difficult to find an instance of divine worship, even of the Father, recorded in the word of God? These are only samples of numerous passages that might be quoted from the New Testament, showing that divine honor was paid to the Christ, when he was on earth, in form and fashion as a man, "the son of man" as well as "the son of God."

Turning now to the Old Testament, and keeping in mind that the Word was the Executive Deity, that he was one of the Elohim, one of the "our" and "us" engaged in the creation, that his most common name was Jehovah, we find that all the worship there recorded, while it included the Supreme and Infinite ONE, as our worship of him also must, included him also. Nor is the Father in any sense or in any degree compromised by the worship of the Son. Jesus himself has placed that matter beyond doubt and beyond cavil, when he says, John v, 23, "He hath given all judgment unto the Son; that all may honor the Son, even as they honor the Father. He that honoreth not the Son, honoreth not the Father that sent him." It must also be conceded that obedience to God can in no way or degree compromise or detract from his honor or dignity, as Supreme Sovereign; and we read, Heb. i, 6, "When he bringeth in the firstbegotten into the world, he saith, 'And let all the angels of God worship him.'" In the 8th verse we also read, "Of the Son he saith, 'Thy throne, O God, is for ever and ever.'" If the Father calls the Son "God," and commands the angels to worship him, can we doubt the propriety of calling him by the same name, and rendering him the same worship? Let us exclaim, then, with Thomas, John xx, 28, "My Lord and my God."

There is, also, one event recorded in the Old Testament, that is, to my mind, significantly allegorical, as illustrating the position of the Son, in the divine economy of the universe, and government of the kingdom of God. Turn to Genesis xli, 40-44, "And Pharaoh said unto Joseph, Thou shalt be over my house, and according to thy word shall all my people be ruled: only in the throne will I be greater than thou. * * * And Pharaoh took off the ring from his hand, and put it upon Joseph's hand, and arrayed him in vestures of fine linen, and put a gold chain about his neck; and he made him to ride in the second chariot which he had; and they cried before him, Bow the knee; and he made him ruler over all the land of Egypt." The instructive points in this transaction are:

First, Joseph's authority in the kingdom was absolute, with the one exception of Pharaoh himself. It included even "my house," the members of his family, as well as "all my people." Joseph was accountable directly to Pharaoh, and to him alone. This authority was so absolute and unlimited that Pharaoh did not reserve even the right of appeal to himself from Joseph's decisions. When Judah plead before Joseph for the release of Benjamin, he recognized this fact by saying, Gen. xliv, 18, "For thou art even as Pharaoh;" the import of which plainly is, If I win not my case before you, it is hopeless; there is no appeal to Pharaoh.

Secondly, Joseph held no part of that authority in his own right. It was all conferred upon him by Pharaoh.

Thirdly, In rendering royal honor to Joseph, in accordance with the command of Pharaoh, the people honored Pharaoh even as they honored Joseph.

This transaction illustrates precisely, according to my understanding, the relations of the Son both to the Father and to all the other intelligences in the whole universe, the universal kingdom of God. With this conception of the situation, and of the nature of worship, no one can doubt for an instant the right of the Son to receive, and the duty of men as well as angels to render to him divine honor and worship. Many other passages might be quoted, and many other phases of the argument presented, but we regard the above as convincing, unanswerable and all sufficient. "If they hear not Moses and the prophets, neither will they be persuaded, if one rise from the dead."

THE HOLY SPIRIT.

I. The personality of the Holy Spirit.

Jesus says, "John iv, 24, "God is a Spirit." We read, respecting angels, Heb. i, 14, "Are they not all ministering spirits?" and in Heb. xii, 23, "Spirits of just men made perfect." Demons are also called "evil spirits," "unclean spirits," etc. These passages are conclusive on the question, whether the word spirit may designate personality. We find it applied to every class of personalities of which we have knowledge. We find, also, in innumerable passages of Scripture, that God is Holy. Since, then, God is a Spirit, and is also Holy, is it not eminently fitting that he should be called, by way of pre-eminence, "The Holy Spirit?"

Again. No one, to whom the Scriptures are the inspired word of God, doubts that God, the first person in the Godhead, was the Father of our Lord Jesus Christ. On this ground he is called "God the Father." Nor can there be any possible evasion of the fact that the Holy Spirit is the Father of our Lord Jesus Christ. Read Luke i, 35, "The Holy Spirit shall come upon thee, and the power of the Most High shall overshadow thee, wherefore also the holy thing which is begotten shall be called the Son of God;" also Mat. i, 20, "Joseph, thou son of David, fear not to take unto thee Mary, thy wife; for that which is conceived in her is of the Holy Spirit." The inevitable logical conclusion is that The Holy Spirit is God the Father. Two other conclusions follow this with equal positiveness and certainty: The Holy Spirit is a person, for paternity implies personality; and he is the First Person in the Godhead, for God the Father is the First Person. Moreover, he is the One and the only Self-existent and Eternal God.

The above are propositions from which,

to a believer in the Word of God, there is no escape, and of which successful evasion is impossible. The logic of the argument is faultless; the truth of the premises, indisputable; and the only thing that can hinder the assent of any reader will be the prejudice that is begotten of a previous theory, or of no theory at all.

The conclusions here reached also illustrate how strict adherence to Bible statements and Bible logic is able to reconcile doctrinal differences that have long been considered unreconcilable, though plain Scriptural statements seemed to support each of the conflicting theories.

The point of contention between those who advocate and those who deny the personality of the Holy Spirit has been this: Its advocates, failing to observe what I have shown above, have contended that he was a third person; while its opposers, through the same failure, have seen no other way to maintain their denial of tri-personality in the Godhead than to deny the personality of the Holy Spirit entirely. The latter refuse to give due weight to such passages as plainly teach personality, because they will not be driven to a conclusion, for which they find neither necessity in the nature of providential methods, nor substantial evidence in the inspired word. The former fail to see that the Holy Spirit, when designating a person, may always be referred to the Father, and that to contend that the reference is to a third person necessitates the absurdity of supposing there are two separate persons in the Godhead, each of whom is designated by the appellation Holy Spirit.

Surely no candid inquirer after truth can reasonably maintain that there are two persons in the Godhead, to each of whom this appellation is applied. That it can with perfect propriety be applied to the Father, and that the Holy Spirit is the Father of the Son of Mary, are statements that cannot be disputed without a plain contradiction of the divine record. There is no fact more plainly and positively taught in the Bible than that the Holy Spirit is the Father of the son of Mary, and hence, must be God the Father—the first person in the Godhead.

In the light of the foregoing, each party to this controversy can accept the Scripture teaching, that the Holy Spirit is the First Person in the Godhead, thereby admitting his personality; and from that standpoint both will be prepared to understand alike all the teaching of the Scriptures respecting him. The word trinity, inexplicable and mysterious, as well as unscriptural, as applied to the Godhead, will drop out of the vocabulary of theological dogmas; vain attempts to explain the inexplicable mystery will cease forever; one of the most bitter and uncharitable of all the controversies that have agitated and irritated the followers of the Prince of Peace, and hindered the progress and triumph of truth and righteousness in the earth, will come to a perpetual end; and one of the worst of all the barbed-wire fences that ever separated the sheep of the Good Shepherd will be broken down and destroyed forever.

II. The phrase Holy Spirit is often used in the Scriptures to express divine influence, energy, power. Personality, however, is always implied as the source of such influence, energy or power. Luke xxiv. 49, "Tarry ye in the city until ye be clothed with power from on high." Acts i. 8, "Ye shall receive power, when the Holy Spirit is come upon you." Acts i. 5, "John indeed baptised with water, but ye shall be baptized in the Holy Spirit not many days hence." The apostles' understanding of these instructions and promises is fairly inferable from the course they pursued immediately after the ascension, and the extraordinary events that transpired on and subsequent to the day of Pentecost. Since, however, this was not the beginning of the efficient agency of the Holy Spirit, let us study its phenomena in the earlier history of our race. The first reference on record to the influence of the Holy Spirit upon men is found in Gen. vi. 3, "And Jehovah said, My Spirit shall not strive with man forever." Here, in the very infancy of the human race, is an unmistakable recognition of the fact that God exerted a mysterious influence, not coercive but persuasive, upon the hearts and lives of men.

Have we any means by which we can

form an idea, a rational conception of what that influence is and how it is exerted? Let us see. Man was created in the image of his Creator. Since this influence evinces an intimate relationship between man and God, may there not be something in man that bears a close resemblance to this mysterious power that God manifestly exerts upon his creature man? something that puts the two in touch, each with the other, thus effecting responsive action between them. Men have a peculiar and mysterious influence over one another. This influence is subtle, indefinable, sometimes attractive, sometimes repulsive, often very powerful, and belongs to every member of the human family, but not in the same degree to each. It is not limited to spoken words, material contact, or even visible presence. The name by which we designate this subtle power is magnetism; probably because of its many points of resemblance to what is called magnetism in matter.

Now, no one would dare maintain that God has given to man a power or faculty that he does not possess himself. Admitting then that God possesses and exerts over men a magnetic power or influence, is it manifested in any other way than that known to us as the Holy Spirit? No intimation of any other magnetic influence over men, from a divine source, is found in the Scriptures; and no man has ever been aware of any such influence, other than this, in his personal experiences. What other conclusion then can we come to than that this subtle, indescribable influence, exerted by God upon the souls and lives of men, is the Divine magnetism? This magnetic contact is the channel of an intercommunion of thought and feeling that we call "the fellowship of the Spirit," and which is also of the same nature as our "fellowship one with another."

III. A partial enumeration of the effects wrought upon men, in different ages, by the Holy Spirit, is now in order.

1. From the text already quoted, Gen. vi. 3 "My spirit shall not strive with man forever," we learn that one of the uses of this divine magnetism, called the Holy Spirit, is to influence men to do that which

is right and pleasing in the sight of God. This work of the Spirit is recognized in Ps. li. 11, "Take not thy Holy Spirit from me." Gal. v. 16, "Walk by the Spirit, and ye shall not fulfill the lust of the flesh." Rom. viii. 1, "Walk not after the flesh, but after the Spirit;" ·Eph. iv. 30, "Grieve not the Holy Spirit of God;" Mark iii. 29, "Whosoever shall blaspheme against the Holy Spirit hath never forgiveness;" and in a multitude of other passages. The truth is, men are dependent upon the Holy Spirit, directly or indirectly, for every good impulse they ever experience, for every influence that leads them upward as individuals and that elevates the race to better conditions. "No man can come to me, except the Father that sent me draw him" (John vi. 44). Valuable and important as learning and society may be, for the growth and developement of desirable mental and social qualities of character, nothing but moral influences, influences that come to us from the Holy Spirit, through our own spiritual nature, truly elevate the soul, and establish and maintain our true and heaven-designed relations with God, securing in us the state, and for us the end, for which our being has been given us.

2. For the gift of prophecy, the inspiration that reveals to the finite mind events that lie in the long distant future, we always have been and ever must be dependent upon divine revelation. He alone, who knows the end from the beginning, has predicted, or can with any certainty predict the future. The same is also true in regard to events that have transpired or will transpire in heaven, and that transpired on earth before the creation of man. This also is the work of the Holy Spirit. "For no prophecy ever came by the will of man; but men spake from God, being moved by the Holy Spirit" (2 Pet. i. 21; 1 Pet. i. 10, 11).

3. For the inspiration that gives the humble follower of Christ bravery in the face of danger, boldness in the declaration of unwelcome truth, steadfastness in the line of a difficult duty, we may depend upon the Holy Spirit, through whose agency the promise is fulfilled, "My grace is sufficient for you." This is the grace that has been

vouchsafed in all ages. Noah experienced it in his day. It sustained Elijah when he stood alone among the four hundred prophets of Baal, challenged them to the fiery test, and hewed his way through the terrible scene of carnage and blood that followed. Nathan realized its sustaining power when he said to David, his King, "Thou art the man." Daniel trusted in it when he stood before the kings of Babylon, and rebuked their impiety; also when he refused to recognize or pray to any god but the God of Israel. Peter was emboldened by it when, a prisoner before the Sanhedrin, "filled with the Holy Spirit," he made a plea that, for bold defiance and crushing effect upon his malicious judges, surpassed all similar pleas ever made at the bar. Acts iv. 8--12, "By the name of Jesus Christ of Nazareth, whom ye crucified, whom God raised from the dead, even in him doth this man stand here before you whole. He is the stone which was set at nought of you builders, which was made the head of the corner. And in none other is there salvation, and neither is there any other name under heaven that is given among men wherein we must be saved." The secret of the boldness, energy, defiance, and crushing power of this plea is revealed in the words, "filled with the Holy Spirit." The boldness and power of Paul and others, on various occasions was inspired by the same agency.

4. Another form in which "the inspiration of the Almighty giveth them understanding" was experienced by the apostles on the day of Pentecost, (Acts ii. 2-4). Its striking manifestations were, "Suddenly there came from heaven a sound as of the rushing of a mighty wind; . . . there appeared unto them tongues parting asunder, like as of fire; . . . and they began to speak with other tongues." The cause assigned for all this is, "They were all filled with the Holy Spirit; . . . the Spirit gave them utterance."

The gift of healing, and of working other miracles, that seems not to have been an abiding and conscious power, but came upon the apostles as occasion required; such as the healing of the lame man at the gate of the temple (Acts iii. 1-6), and the raising of

Dorcas to life by Peter (Acts ix. 39-41); the healing of the cripple at Lystra (Acts xiv. 8-10), and the raising to life of Eutichus at Troas (Acts xx. 10), by Paul; and many other works requiring miraculous agency are of the same nature. They are found in the catalogue of "spiritual gifts," given by Paul, 1 Cor. xii.

Nor did these divine magnetic forces, sometimes miraculous and sometimes only giving extraordinary activity and power to natural endowments, leave the world with the apostles. Martin Luther, John Knox, Jonathan Edwards, Asahel Nettleton, Charles G. Finney, Dwight L. Moody, and hundreds of others, from the days of the apostles to the present time, have been instructed, inspired, emboldened and energized, in ways diverse and innumerable, by the same supernatural and divine agency. If this is not the case, these men were all mistaken themselves, for without exception they believed that the Divine hand was leading them and the Divine Spirit enlightening and inspiring them, thus giving their labors supernatural efficiency.

5. There is another sense in which the word spirit is used that may be helpful to us in getting a true and clear conception of the nature and working of the Holy Spirit. The remark is often made, "I like his spirit," or "I do not like his spirit." There are tones of voice, movements of the head and body, gestures and attitudes, that seem to us to indicate constitutional dispositions, permanent or temporary states of mind, that we employ the word spirit to designate, judging the inner by the outer man. This spirit is very potent in its influence over others. It is very apt to produce its like in others, with whom it comes in contact. It is reported of a New England minister, of nearly a hundred years ago, that he used to say, "I do not want to be a bigot; I hate a bigot; but when I am talking with a bigot, I become a bigot myself, before I am aware of it."

An amiable, gentle, loving disposition is influential to generate its like in others by the same law. This influence is magnetic, and illustrates how the dispositions of the divine mind are reproduced in the minds of those who have been made "partakers of the divine nature." It is thus that communion with God, by a natural law, comforts the disconsolate, strengthens the weak, imparts supernatural vigor of mind to perceive truth, and force of utterance to express it; gives fortitude to endure pain, persecution, false accusation, malicious opposition; and grace in any form that the exigencies of an occasion may demand, whether in life or in death. Here we find also, in one form, the reasonableness and efficacy of prayer.

6. The figures of speech employed to express the working of the Holy Spirit upon the hearts and lives of men are often very suggestive of its nature, and demonstrative that influence instead of personality is meant.

Passages of this kind are numerous. Only a few will be quoted. Prov. i. 23, "Behold I will pour out my Spirit unto you;" Isa. xliv. 3, "I will pour my Spirit upon thy seed, and my blessing upon thine offspring;" Isa. xxxii. 15, "Until the Spirit be poured upon us from on high, and the wilderness become a fruitful field;" Joel ii. 28, 29, quoted by Peter Acts ii. 17, 18, "It shall come to pass afterward, that I will pour out my spirit upon all flesh, and your sons and your daughters shall prophecy, your old men shall dream dreams, your young men shall see visions; and also upon the servants and upon the handmaids, in those days, will I pour out my spirit."

That the word spirit (and it is God's spirit every time), in these quotations, represents an influence instead of a personality, is so evident from the connection and scope of the passages that the translators, both of the old and new versions, have used a small instead of a capital S in spelling the word. The truth is, while this figure of speech, to pour out, is very appropriate and expressive in many other connections, especially to represent the magnetic power one earnest person may exert upon another, the idea of pouring one person upon another is inconceivable. An influence, a feeling, the magnetic power of one person over another, is itself suggestive of a fluid that may be poured, but a conception of personality forbids it.

7. The idea of being filled with the Holy Spirit, as employed many times, par-

ticularly in the Acts of the Apostles, is of the same nature. Take the following as samples:—Acts ii. 2, "They were all filled with the Holy Spirit, and began to speak with other tongues, as the Spirit gave them utterance;" iv. 31, "They were all filled with the Holy Spirit, and they spake the word of God with boldness;" vi. 5, "They chose Stephen, a man full of faith and of the Holy Spirit;" xiii. 9, "Saul, who is also called Paul, filled with the Holy Spirit, fastened his eyes on him," etc.; Luke iv. 1, "Jesus, full of the Holy Spirit, returned from the Jordan." No one can fail to see that Holy Spirit, in these passages, can have no other signification than a divine enthusiasm, giving them quickness of perception and discernment, great courage and boldness and fitness for their work, and a magnetic influence over others that brooked no resistance.

8. Whence does this divine spirit, influence, power, proceed? where is the fountain head out of which it all flows? That its origin is a personal intelligence is evident from its nature. It is exerted upon intelligent be-

ings, and its effects are intelligent in the highest degree. The question we want to come at is, Is it exerted by the Father alone, or by both the Father and the Son? This question has been in dispute between the Greek and the Roman churches ever since the Council of Nice, A. D. 325; the Greek church contending that it proceeds from the Father only; the Roman maintaining that it proceeds from the Father and the Son. The Scriptures that bear upon the question are the following:—John xiv. 16, "I will pray the Father and he shall give you another Comforter;" verse 26, "The Comforter, even the Holy Spirit, whom the Father will send in my name, he shall teach you all things, and bring to your remembrance all that I said unto you;" John xv. 26, "When the Comforter is come, whom I will send unto you from the Father, even the Spirit of truth, which proceedeth from the Father, he shall bear witness of me;" John xvi. 7, "It is expedient for you that I go away; for if I go not away, the Comforter will not come unto you; but if I go, I will send him unto you." These are the only passages that bear directly upon the question. What would these passages teach to an unprejudiced mind? to one who had no previously adopted theory to maintain? to one who did not know that any dispute had ever existed respecting it, and in whose mind the question had just arisen for the first time? It seems to me the answer must be plain to every candid mind. Let us see. He reads, "I will pray the Father, and he shall give you." Could he get any other idea from this than that the thing spoken of was found in the Father, was at his disposal, and would be given on request of the Son? He reads again, "Whom the father will send in my name." This would strengthen his first impression. Again he reads, "Whom I will send unto you from the Father." The Son promises to send the Comforter; but still recognizes the Father as the source whence he will come. He reads further, "Even the Spirit of truth, which proceedeth from the Father." The question is settled. There is no room for doubt. The source, whence this hallowed influence—this Holy

Spirit—emanates is the Father; and why not, since he is the source of all things? He reads once more, "If I go, I will send him unto you." His opinion is not changed, for he remembers the other passage, where he read, "I will send him unto you from the Father." Omitting reference, in a single instance, to the source, is not construed as claiming to be the source himself, since he had just stated that it belonged only to the Father.

Now, on the hypothesis that we have assumed, that these phrases, "the Comforter," "the Spirit of truth," "the Holy Spirit," in the passages under consideration, refer to the influence that we have called the divine magnetism, the doctrine of the passages plainly is that, while the Father is the original source, the fountain head, of this wonderful "power from on high," it is also, by the will of the Father, exercised by, and at the disposal of, the Son, "in whom dwelleth all the fullness of the Godhead," (Col. ii. 8); "for it pleased the Father that in him should all fullness dwell." (Col. i. 19).

This is also in perfect accord with the uniform teaching of the Son himself, respecting the powers and authority possessed by him. "All power in heaven and on earth is given unto me of the Father" is his oft repeated declaration, in regard to both his works and words. This power to confer the Spirit on whom he chose corresponds precisely with, and is fully explained by, his statement, John v. 26, "As the Father hath life in himself, even so gave he to the Son also to have life in himself." Thus, having this power, by the will of the Father, the Spirit proceeded from him when "he breathed upon them (the disciples), and said, Receive ye the Holy Spirit," (John xx. 22).

Furthermore, inasmuch as every other intelligence in the world, whether human or angelic, is endowed by the Creator with a similar magnetic power, it follows that each one is capable of exerting an influence, good or bad according to the Spirit that is in him. This accounts for the incident that occurred at Ephesus, Acts xix., when Paul found there certain disciples who, when "baptized into John's baptism," "did not so much as hear whether the Holy Spirit was;" but having been baptized "into the name of the Lord Jesus," "when Paul had laid his hands upon them, the Holy Spirit came on them." A similar event occurred also while Peter was preaching to the household of Cornelius (Acts x. 44), "The Holy Spirit fell on them who heard the word." Being filled with the Holy Spirit himself, Peter imparted the same to his hearers.

8. There is yet one circumstance of very great significance and importance, as to its bearing upon the question of the third-personality of the Holy Spirit. While the Father and the Son often speak, as self-conscious persons, using the personal pronouns of the first person—I, we, us—under circumstances that exclude the possibility of a mistake as to their personality; and while they are often addressed in the second person, prayer and praise and prostrate worship offered to them, every mention of the Holy Spirit is in the third person. Gen. vi. 3 does not read, The Holy Spirit said, I will not strive with man forever. In Ps. li.

11, David does not pray, Holy Spirit, do not leave me. Nor is there any thing similar to these forms of expression any where in the word of God. Jehovah said, "My Spirit shall not strive with man forever." David said, "Take not thy Holy Spirit from me."

An apparent exception to this affirmation is found in Acts xiii. 2, "The Holy Spirit said, Separate me Barnabas and Saul, for the work whereunto I have called them." The meaning and intent of these words manifestly are not to state that the Holy Spirit was there in person, giving directions as to the setting apart of these men, but that there was a suggestion to their minds, which they recognized as from above, moving them to that act. The pronouns I and me refer to the person from whom the suggestion came—manifestly from Jesus himself. The same interpretation is to be given to Acts xvi. 6, "having been forbidden of the Holy Spirit to preach the word in Asia," and to a large number of similar passages in the New Testament.

If the Holy Spirit were a separate, self-conscious, self-determining third personality, to whom was assigned a specific work, to be effected through his individual, personal agency, a work to which he assented, and in which he engaged of his own free will and accord, and for which he was individually responsible and accountable, as is clearly the case with the Son, and with every other moral agent, is it not reasonable to suppose that he would often have spoken and acted in his own individual capacity? ascribing his authority and power to the Father, as the Son so uniformly did? A single intimation from him that he came forth from the Father, and that the Father sent him, both giving him authority and imparting to him ability to do the work assigned him, would have placed this whole question of personality in the clear sunlight of certainty. Is not the absence of all such claims at least suggestive of non-personality?

9. Another significant inquiry arises in my mind, Why has the Holy Spirit, if a third personality, having so much to do with men as is ascribed to him, never made a visible appearance to any human eye? An-

gels, who are "ministering spirits," have been frequently seen by human eyes; saints, "the spirits of just men made perfect," were seen on the mount of transfiguration; Jehovah, the impersonated Word, talked with Moses "face to face;" but the Holy Spirit has never been seen by any one, never spoke an audible word to anybody; and there is no record that he ever appeared to any one even in a dream, or vision.

Moreover, when John had his wonderful vision of the heavenly world and its inhabitants, from the Isle of Patmos, he saw every other form of personality of whom we have ever heard, not excepting "him that sat upon the throne," from whose hand "the Lion of the tribe of Judah," "the Lamb that was slain" (Rev. v.), took the book; but makes no mention of the Holy Spirit. John saw distinctly the Father and the Son, but makes no mention of the Holy Spirit.

Still further, John says, Rev. v. 13, "And every created thing which is in heaven, and on the earth, and under the earth, and on the sea, and all things that are in them, heard I saying, Unto him that sitteth on the throne, and unto the Lamb, be the blessing, and the honor, and the glory, and the dominion, for ever and ever;" but there is not a word ascribing glory, or praise, or honor, or power, to the Holy Spirit, neither in this passage, nor in any other passage in the whole book of Revelation, nor anywhere else in the Bible. If there was a personal Holy Spirit, in heaven or on earth, no "revelation" of the fact was ever made to John. He never knew any thing about it. In his first epistle, i. 3, he says, "Our fellowship is with the Father and with his Son Jesus Christ;" but not a word about fellowship with the Holy Spirit. This fact appears the more strange and unaccountable, because of the important works attributed to that agency, throughout the New Testament. It is simply impossible that one of the persons of the Godhead, who had performed so important a part in the work of saving the souls of the millions that John saw, should be unrecognized, unnoticed, unmentioned, even unseen, in that stupendous vision of the winding up of all earthly things.

Verily, I must believe, my judgment and reason can not decide otherwise, that the doctrine of a third person in the Godhead, designated as the Holy Spirit, is a delusion. To say it is a mystery does not help the matter at all. The mystery is too great. It is nothing less than impossible. Those who believe and advocate it are undoubtedly sincere, but they are surely mistaken. Reader, do not anathematize me, as many have often done, for disbelieving the dogma. Extend to me the same charity that I extend to you. You can not be more fully, candidly, honestly convinced in your judgment than I am in mine. In fact, I believe that, if you will lay aside the prejudices in which you have been educated, and examine the question thoroughly, *de novo*, you will come to the same conclusion as I have. Dare to think for yourself. Dare to investigate. Dare to believe. Dare to express your belief. "When he, the Spirit of truth, is come, he shall guide you into all truth." Willingness to know truth is the open door into which truth delights to enter.

OBJECTIONS ANSWERED.

Of passages that seem to conflict with these views, two only need explanation. These are Mat. xxviii. 19, "Baptizing them into the name of the Father and of the Son and of the Holy Spirit;" and 2 Cor. xiii. 14, "The grace of our Lord Jesus Christ, and the love of God, and the communion of the Holy Spirit, be with you." As for this latter passage, its language is sufficient explanation. Personality is without doubt implied in the exercise of grace and love. Only a person can show favor, and only a person can love. "Communion of the Holy Spirit" is quite a different matter. The word "communion" can convey no other idea than an exchange of kindly feelings, pleasing emotions, that "flow of soul" that is experienced by persons who are on intimate and loving terms with one another, a harmonious confluence of sweet sympathies, precisely of the nature expressed in 1 John i. 3, "Our fellowship is with the Father and with his Son Jesus Christ." The meaning of the benediction is, The grace of our Lord Jesus Christ be with you;

the love of God be with you; and the sweet consciousness of the indwelling of the divine presence be with you.

The formula of baptism may not be quite so easily disposed of; and were it not for the plain teaching of both Scripture and reason, as presented in this discussion, might easily be accepted as including three personalities. A different construction is, however, neither difficult nor unnatural, and is demanded by facts and passages already considered. Its object manifestly is, at that solemn moment, when the candidate is in the act of putting on Christ "through baptism into death," to remind him of the three agencies by which those who are dead "through trespasses and sins" may be "made alive" and permanently saved from their thraldom and power. These are the same as are referred to in the benediction above; "the love of God," who devised the plan; "the grace of our Lord Jesus Christ," who "for our sakes became poor," who "gave himself a ransom for many," who "suffered for sin once, the righteous for the unrighteous, that he might bring us to God;" and that divinely magnetic, enlightening, inspiring, sustaining, strengthening influence that comes from "fellowship with the Father and with his Son Jesus Christ." In the act of baptism, he proclaims to the world his trust in these agencies for his own salvation and the salvation of the world. These are the divine, supernatural agencies on which every man must depend, who would escape from the guilt and bondage of sin, become reconciled to God, enabled to accomplish the mission on which he has been sent into this world, and gain the everlasting favor of both the Father and the Son in the world to come.

LECTURE X.

ETERNAL PUNISHMENT

That moral agents may persist in sin, resisting every saving influence that can be brought to bear upon them, until they attain a fixedness of purpose, a willful and unalterable attitude of rebellion against God, against truth, against light, against every means of saving grace, has been shown repeatedly in the preceding lectures. My object in this lecture is to show more fully the working of this great and solemn fact, to show also that the Scriptures teach, and reason sustains, with great positiveness, what the nature of moral agency renders possible; namely, that in certain cases human souls do acquire such an attitude, and thereby incur certainly and inevitably their own eternal ruin.

As a basis of our argument, I assume as axiomatic the following propositions:

1. On all questions of eschatology, on which the Son of God himself has spoken,

his utterances, rightly interpreted, are final authority.

2. On questions, respecting which the Son of God is silent, the affirmations of reason, when undeniably logical, may be taken as reliable, providing always that they do not conflict with plain, unequivocal statements of the inspired word. Such conflict is evidence of faulty reasoning, not of unreliable Scripture.

Before entering upon our argument proper, it is very important that we rid ourselves of a very great and blinding error, of long standing and almost universal prevalence. Shocking and terrible as the very thought is, most Christians will admit, at this very hour, that they believe that it is the decree of heaven that, for the commission of a single sin, the transgression of a single law, the omission of a single duty, eternal banishment from God and heaven may justly follow. Some there are, good men and true, who recognize the terribleness of the thought, and wonder how it can be that divine justice has affixed to a single act of neglect of duty the same penalty as to life-long devotion to most reckless, diabolical crime. Still others, not the worst men in the world by any means, impelled by a sense of outraged justice, and presuming that the Bible teaches such a doctrine, reject the whole system of Christianity, Bible included, and declare themselves outspoken and uncompromising infidels.

This is one of the dark places into which acquaintance with the nature and principles of moral agency will throw a flood of light. In order to throw open the window, and let in light upon this subject, we advance a proposition that will undoubtedly startle some even of our thoughtful readers. It is this: The commission of a single sin, or of any number of sins, from the neglect of a thoughtless child to obey a trivial requirement of a parent, to the commission of the most heinous crime, is not the damning act that seals the everlasting doom of the lost soul. If it were, the doom would be sealed from the moment the act was committed. All talk of mercy would be idle. The gospel would be meaningless; or, rather, there would be no gospel. Impenetrable darkness, hopeless despair, would fall upon the offender like a pall of blackest midnight, without a ray from the faintest star, the moment he became conscious of his offense.

Such, however, is not the case. The call to repentance, the offer of pardon and restoration to the favor of God, mean there is yet hope. You are a sinner indeed, your guilt is great, you are "condemned already," but not to eternal despair, unless you commit another act, in addition to the sins already committed, an act of sin whose enormity is immeasurable, inexpressible, irretrievable. That act is simply refusal to repent. By that act, with your own hand, you close the door of hope that a merciful Savior has thrown wide open before you. By that act, of your own free will, you refuse to yield to the only influence, the least and the greatest; refuse to accept the only means, the first and the last and all between, by which the bondage of sin can be broken. After that fatal decision, no means can be found, in heaven to invite, in earth to persuade, or in hell to warn and terrify, that you have not resisted and overcome.

How are you then to be brought to repentance, that you may be saved? By that dreadful decision, you deliberately form a fixed purpose, not that you can not but that you will never change—a final choice. By that act you banish the Holy Spirit from your heart forever, turn the warnings of conscience into the scorpion stings of remorse, and enthrone Satan in your soul as your king and sovereign, swearing loyalty to him for all eternity, and renouncing all allegiance to God your rightful Sovereign, and Jesus your only Savior. You have often asked, What is the sin against the Holy Spirit? It is this very refusal to yield to the persuasions of Infinite Love, the appeals of the sufferings and death of the Divine Son of God, the tears, entreaties and prayers of Christian friends — the best friends you have on earth. "Verily I say unto you, All their sins shall be forgiven unto the sons of men, and their blasphemies wherewith soever they shall blaspheme; but whosoever shall blaspheme against the Holy Spirit hath never forgiveness, but is guilty of an eternal sin" (Mark iii. 28, 29).

Note well "an eternal sin." This is the correct translation of the very words of Jesus.

Eternal punishment means eternal sin. It is not the penalty of a single act of inadvertent, nor of deliberately intentional, disobedience. It is the deliberate and intentional re-enactment of that sin; the deliberate perpetuation of that sinful, disloyal, rebellious state of heart and will, that resists, repels, with unyielding, eternally persistent purpose, every good and saving influence; and gives itself up to every debasing desire, every diabolical pursuit, into which the great enemy of all righteousness may lead. It was of such that Jesus said, John viii. 44, "Ye are of your father the devil, and the lusts of your father it is your will to do." Thus the impenitent, unrepentant sinner seals his own doom, and seals it for eternity; in spite of all the means that Infinite Love can prompt, Infinite Wisdom devise, Infinite Mercy present. Who shall deny the eternity of his punishment, when he persists eternally in sin? Who shall charge God with cruelty, or unkindness, or even indifference, under such a state of things? Hear his own declaration respecting it; Ezek. xxxiii. 11, "As I live, saith the Lord God, I have no pleasure in the death of the wicked; but that the wicked turn from his way and live; turn ye, turn ye, from your evil ways, for why will ye die?" Such is the light in which the facts of moral agency place the question of eternal punishment. Thus the sinner seals his own doom. The door of his heart is closed against Mercy; because he has himself bolted it, and keeps it bolted by his persistent determination not to let Mercy in to cleanse him from sin, and save him from eternal punishment.

Thus far, in this lecture, we have only shown that the philosophy of moral agency reveals the possibility of souls sinning away the day of grace, and sealing their doom to eternal despair. This does not prove that any have ever done this, are doing it now, or ever will do it. Potentialities do not always indicate actualities or certainties. Holy angels, being moral agents, are competent to sin, though their fixed character for holiness, their final choice of loyalty to

God, assures us that they never will. Demons also, being still moral agents, are competent to repent, but their fixed character for rebellion against God, their final choice of eternal alienation from him, render it certain that they never will. So the fact that men, all men, may separate themselves forever from holiness and heaven, is also the fact that they may, all of them, take the unalterable oath, make the final choice, to stand by the banner of the cross, "fight the good fight of faith, and lay hold of the life eternal." Our question now is, Do any, have any, will any fail of doing this?

This is a question the most logical reasoning can not answer. It is a question of fact; and the facts in the case can be known only to those who are acquainted with the affairs of the spirit-world as well as with the events that have transpired, are transpiring, and will transpire, not only in the outward lives but in the most secret recesses of the souls of men here on earth. Such beings there are. The Uncaused Cause of all things knows the end from the beginning. "The only begotten Son, who is in the bosom of the Father," who speaks of the glory he had with the Father before the world was, who "needed not that any one should bear witness concerning man, for he himself knew what was in man,"—these know all the facts in the case. Have they spoken? They surely have. Shall we listen to their utterances? May the Spirit of truth help us that we may both hear and believe. Of the many passages of the inspired word that might be cited a few will suffice. One word from these sources is as good as a thousand.

Turn directly to Mat. xxv. 46, "These shall go away into eternal punishment, but the righteous into eternal life." This most positive statement as to the facts in this case is from the lips of the Son of God, and, interpreted in the light of its connection, can not, as it appears to me, be honestly misunderstood. Words can not be made to express a more clear, unequivocal, unpervertible statement on any subject. The occasion is the final judgment. The sentence was, verse 41, "Depart from me, ye cursed, into the eternal fire which is prepared for the devil and his angels." The indictment was, verse 42, "for I was an hungered, and ye gave me no meat; I was thirsty, and ye gave me no drink; I was a stranger, and ye took me not in; naked, and ye clothed me not; sick, and in prison, and ye visited me not." This means that they had failed to discharge the duties of man to his fellow man, in the circumstances supposed; they had not obeyed the law of love, and done to others as they would that others should do to them, and includes the circumstance that, when called to repentance for their sin, they had refused to do that.

This one passage is sufficient to establish the fact in question; but, on account of changed circumstances, we cite one more. Speaking of the self-sacrifices one should make, even of the most important members of the body, rather than be led into sin by them, he says, Mark ix. 47, 48, "It is good for thee to enter into the kingdom of God with one eye, rather that having two eyes to be cast into hell (not hades but gehenna), where their worm dieth not, and the fire is not quenched."

According to these straight forward, positive, unequivocal passages, from the highest authority, there are two forms of sin—neglect of duties to our fellow men, and refusal to practice necessary self-denial, a duty we owe ourselves—that, unrepented, incur the everlasting displeasure of God. It follows, therefore, from the positive statements of the Son of God, that men, in this life, not only may but actually do seal their own doom to eternal despair.

In mathematics it is often, perhaps always, possible to reach correct results by different processes of reasoning, each process thus proving the correctness of the result, as well as the soundness of the argument, in the other. We have another argument, equally Scriptural with the above, and with larger, though not better, show of logic, that clearly demonstrates the same conclusion. It is based on the usage of the words life and death.

We read, Rom. vi. 23, "The wages of sin is death." We read again, Isa. lix. 2, "Your iniquities have separated between you and your God, and your sins have hid his face from you." In Ps. xxx. 5, we read, "In his favor is life." Referring to the tree of forbidden fruit, in the garden of Eden, God said to our first parents, Gen. ii. 17, "In the day thou eatest thereof thou shalt surely die." The death here threatened was spiritual death. They died no other in the day they ate thereof; but they did lose the favor of God, which is life. They were then dead. In the same manner. "death passed upon all men, for that all have sinned." Now read 1 John v. 11, 12, "This is the record, that God hath given to us eternal life, and this life is in his Son. He that hath the Son hath life; and he that hath not the Son of God hath not life." Again, John iii. 36, "He that believeth on the Son hath eternal life; but he that believeth not the Son shall not see life, but the wrath of God abideth on him." Note well, "shall not see life, but the wrath of God abideth on him." If the soul that is dead is not made alive by "repentance towards God and faith towards our Lord Jesus Christ," will not that death be eternal? and is not eternal death eternal punishment? Remember, Sin is death, and death is hell, whether in this life or the life to come, and eternal sin is eternal hell. Thus this argument, whose refutation I defy, coincides precisely, in its conclusion, with what moral agency declares possible, and the Son of God has declared certain and actual. "He that hath ears to hear, let him hear."

Considering the doctrine of eternal punishment established upon an unshaken and immovable foundation, let us now inquire carefully, Who are the guilty and wretched individuals, for whom, "the blackness of darkness hath been reserved forever?"

By referring to our first argument in this lecture, we find that those concerning whom the declaration is made, "These shall go away into everlasting punishment," are described as having neglected the common civilities and benevolences due to their fellow men, under the divine law of love; "I was an hungered, and ye gave me no meat; I was thirsty, and ye gave me no drink; I was a stranger, and ye took me not in; naked, and ye clothed me not; sick and in prison, and ye visited me not."

Those who are in danger of "the worm that dieth not and the fire that is not quenched," are such as refuse to "abstain from fleshly lusts, which war against the soul." If thine hand, or thy foot, or thine eye, cause thee to stumble, sacrifice them, for it is better to enter into the kingdom of God destitute of these members, than to be led astray by them, and be cast into hell. These are the indulgences that "separated between them and their God," the sins that hid his face from them, through which they lost his favor, which is life.

Taking these references in connection with others that express God's willingness to pardon, and receive again into his favor, all who exercise genuine "repentance towards God and faith towards our Lord Jesus Christ," and also the consequences of refusal to accept salvation on those terms, we logically and safely conclude that "everlasting destruction from the presence of the Lord and the glory of his power," is the portion only of such as, through intentional and stubborn resistance of the persuasive power of divine love and the strivings of the Holy Spirit, have formed an unchangeable fixedness of moral alienation from and rebellion against the merciful Father, and all the benign influences of heaven and earth for their good, and all the well known terrific consequences of their unreasonable and persistent rebellion. They are lost, because they will not be saved. They have deliberately, knowingly, intentionally "chosen death rather than life;" and have thus banished themselves, with persistent purpose, from the presence and favor of a loving and grief-stricken Father, at the very moment when he was in the full exercise of all his infinite attributes for their welfare, their salvation. What can be done to save from eternal despair souls that will not be attracted by the glories of heaven, nor persuaded by the opportunities of earth, nor deterred by the wailings of the lost, from plunging themselves into the bottomless pit of unutterable and inevitable remorse and self-condemnation?

Owing to the fact that they are moral agents, that they are responsible themselves for the choices they make and the courses of life they elect to pursue, coercion was out of the question, and persuasion proved unavailing to save them from their self-determined fate.

The eternal doom of such characters is fixed, not by a heartless edict of their Sovereign, or sentence of their Judge, but by their own insane and stubborn willfulness. Alas! alas! They are lost! irredeemably, unchangeably, irrecoverably lost! Though they are still moral agents, abiding in their deplorable condition voluntarily, and with ever increasing stubbornness and persistence, they surely will never, never, to all eternity, change their dreadful, self-imposed choice and determination. No influence can be brought to bear upon them that they have not already resisted, and overcome, under more favorable circumstances and environment. For them there is no escape from endless misery but annihilation, and that the extinction of their wretched existence may ever come to their relief, however desirable this may seem, can not, though often attempted, be established by a fair construction of the word of God, and we have no other source of information on that point. No act of suicide will furnish the lost soul a way of escape from eternal misery.

Here we leave them in their own self-incurred, self-responsible, self-reproaching wretchedness. Between them and "Abraham's bosom" "there is a great gulf fixed," but it is the gulf of a fixed purpose and character, not of an arbitrary edict of an angry, vengeful God. Sinner, escape for thy life; escape from thyself; lay hold on eternal life.

LECTURE XI.

FUTURE PROBATION.

Moral agency, power to make choice where choice has not already been made, and to change a choice already made, must continue the same in the future as in the present life. The cessation of moral agency would be the cessation of guilt; and the cessation of guilt would, of necessity, in a perfect moral government, be the cessation of punishment. To inflict punishment upon a creature—a soul—that is incapable, by a law of necessity, either of comprehending its justice or of being reformed thereby, would be the same as torturing a brute. Eternal punishment means eternal sin; and eternal sin means eternal moral agency None but a moral agent can sin. On this ground we erect our point of observation, from which to inquire into the question, whether future probation may be among the possibilities of a future existence.

At the very threshold of this inquiry, we want to state distinctly that this question has no bearing upon and is of no significance whatever to those who have made their choices in this life, and settled the question of loyalty or disloyalty to God. That question settled once is settled forever. Whatever possibilities may still be open before those who have made their final choice, will be no more to them than the possibilities that they have already ignored and spurned. The law of the future life, to all such, is found in Rev. xxii. 11, "He that is unrighteous, let him be unrighteous still more; and he that is filthy, let him be made filthy still more; and he that is righteous, let him do righteousness still more; and he that is holy, let him be made holy still more."

Bear in mind also that the final choice is not made, until the question of repentance and submission to God has been distinctly presented and decided, *pro* or *con*. They only are saved who have submitted to the process of regeneration, and become loyal subjects of the kingdom of God, the kingdom of Christ, the kingdom of heaven; and they only are lost who have refused to submit to this process, have rejected the offers of Mercy, have persisted in disloyalty to God, to Christ, to heaven; and thus have become loyal subjects of the devil and the kingdom of darkness.

That many souls, having reached the years of accountability, and doubtless having brought guilt and condemnation upon themselves by wrong doing, have passed into the future life, without having had any well-defined consciousness of sin, or ever having had the faintest degree of true penitence therefor, or ever having formed a definite purpose either to persist in or to forsake sin, or ever having called upon God for pardon of sin and exercised faith in our Lord Jesus Christ that such pardon was granted, or having received the witness of the Spirit that they were accepted children of God, all of which we consider as unalterable conditions of salvation and eternal life, must undoubtedly be freely and unequivocally admitted.

This class is very large. It will include multitudes of children of Christian and unchristian parents in gospel lands, and still greater multitudes in heathen lands, many of whom never heard the name of him who was called Jesus, "because he should save his people from their sins;" and others of whom have only known of him by the hearing of the ear. Are these all lost? eternally and justly lost?

At this point of our inquiry, whither shall we turn our eyes, that they may catch one ray of light, which, followed, will lead us out of the dense darkness that surrounds us? Inspiration has lifted the veil that hangs between the present and the future, and let at least some degree of light fall upon all other eschatological questions, but no clear, distinct ray glimmers from the word of God upon this one. Shall we drop it then, and relegate it to the dark regions of the unknowable? thus acknowledging ourselves to be agnostic so far as this question is concerned? Others may be willing to do this, but I am not. The question has been raised, and it must be met. It must be studied in the best light we can bring to bear upon it, and the best conclusion possible must be reached. If independent, logical thinkers are not satisfied with our reasoning and conclusions, we may at least provoke them to further and more successful inquiry.

Nor am I willing to concede that we have no light on the subject, because no ray comes direct from the inspired word. Most of the objects seen in the material world are made visible by reflected rays, and no one doubts the reliability of his vision for that reason. In fact, the inspired word itself is only a mirror, reflecting truth from the great source of truth, the infinite mind. It must be that a careful search will reveal light enough, from some reflector, even on this question, to enable a candid mind to form an opinion having at least some of the characteristics of probability. In this confidence, let us

First, contemplate him who is the self-luminous source of light.

Of the disposition of God to save from sin, and from "the perdition of ungodly men," every human soul, and his abundant ability to save all who do not refuse to be saved, and spurn the mercy and persuasive power of our compassionate Redeemer, we are abundantly assured, and that, before any soul is abandoned to hopelessness and despair, every means that infinite mercy can prompt and infinite wisdom devise to save every soul will have been employed and exhausted, so that, if lost, every intelligence in the universe will acquit the final Judge of the least shade of a suspicion of injustice, in the final judgment pronounced, I think can not and will not be disputed by any one.

Secondly, that the multitude of souls, to which we have referred above, who pass into " the world to come " without having voluntarily and intelligently either accepted or rejected the provisions of the gospel for their cleansing from sin and reconcilation to God, in this life, can be justly classed with the deliberately incorrigible, and consigned to the same final doom, at the final judgment, would be an assumption for the support of which few, at the present day, would claim either the declarations of Scripture or the affirmations of reason. There is no court on earth, and there certainly can be none in heaven, in which a person could be convicted of a crime, in the commission of which, he acted no voluntary part, and of which he had no consciousness. Such a court would condemn the idiotic and insane for crimes that require intelligent "malice aforethought," of which they are utterly incapable. The time was when distinguished theologians taught that God was an arbitrary, irresponsible Sovereign, consulting only his own pleasure, and doing all things for his own glory; but the time has come, and come to stay, when it is understood, with no perplexing shades of doubt about it, that God is thoroughly and always reasonable and benevolent; and every act of his, since the dawn of the first morning of time, has been prompted by the most perfect and unalloyed motive of promoting the welfare of his sentient, and especially of his intelligent, creatures.

As bearing upon this question, it should also be remembered that the commission of sin, however heinous, is not the ground of final condemnation, the crime for which the guilty soul is eternally lost; but the refusal to repent and accept the proffered mercy and pardon, provided for in the redemptive sufferings and death of the holy and divine Son of God. This is the sin against the the Holy Spirit, that hath never forgiveness, neither in this world nor in that which is to to come; and there is no other such sin. On these grounds, both Scriptural and reasonable, we advocate the probability of probation for this class—both an opportunity and inducements to exercise "repentance towards God and faith towards our Lord Jesus Christ," after passing through the gates of death.

There is yet another class, whether larger or smaller than the class above mentioned we do not know, who have passed out of this life before the period of moral agency and accountability had come to them. What shall we say about these? We dislike to dispel the beautiful halos that have so long hung over the little mounds of earth that mark the resting places of devoted mothers' dearest treasures; nor will we dispel them, though we must somewhat change their hues.

As we have already seen, the glories of the heavenly world are for those who have proved their loyalty to truth, to righteousness, to God, either by resisting all forms of temptation to sin, as in the case of the holy angels and the Son of God; or, having sinned, have accepted the conditions on which pardon and restoration to the favor of God are offered, and have thus become overcomers "by the blood of the Lamb and the word of their testimony." Now infants, all who have not reached the age of moral accountability, belong to neither of these classes. They leave this life in the state of innocency, in which every moral agent in the universe must commence or must have commenced his existence; and from which character is formed, either holy or sinful, by the choice that each makes of obedience or disobedience, under conditions that we call probation. In this state of innocency they pass into the future life, into *hades*, the place of departed spirits. Now it appears to me that nothing can be more certain than that probation, under some circumstances, must await them there. Concerning the form or manner of the test of their loyalty, under which they make their choices, and form their character, and the influences for good or evil, that may be brought to bear upon them, I have no means that I am aware of of knowing anything, and hence decline to speculate, or even imagine. Only of one thing am I certain; being moral agents, they must form moral character, which implies probation. The inhabitants of heaven are not simply innocent, they must be holy.

On the first page of this lecture, we have made the statement that eternal punishment means eternal sin; and eternal sin means eternal moral agency. Let me now add, Eternal moral agency means eternal probation; not only for infants and for others who have not positively rejected Christ, but for all. Eternal holiness, which is eternal life, means eternal persistence in the choice of that which is good, in the presence of the possibility of choosing the evil. Eternal sin, which is eternal death, means eternal persistence in the choice of that which is evil, in the presence of the possibility of choosing the good. Either state is always and eternally a voluntary state. Intelligent existence under these circumstances is, in a limited sense, probation. The fact that the purpose is unalterable, to maintain, in the one case a state of loyalty, and in the other a state of disloyalty, to God and the good of being, does not destroy moral agency, and one of the conditions of moral agency is an alternative, and the opportunity to make a choice under an alternative is, in a limited sense, probation. Hence the fact that probation after death is even questioned, is based upon a false assumption, that when the final choice is settled, and character is thus determined, moral agency, and with it probation, comes to a perpetual end.

Of course, at this point, the question will be thrust upon me from every direction. May the lost sinner be saved then? and the saved saint in heaven commit sin and be lost? I answer, Yes they MAY, if they WILL. That, like every thing else connected with their moral character and salvation, will depend upon their choice individually. The whole question is and always will be at their own disposal; and each will be accountable for the disposition he makes of his own case. And let me add, This is just as true of angels, the holy and the fallen, and of every other moral agent in the universe, including God himself, as it is of our own race.

Here we have an interminable opportunity to change, coupled with an interminable certainty that no change will ever be made. While some may dispute that this is, in the strictest sense, probation, because of the absence of solicitation, no one will deny that it is at least an invitation, which may be accepted or rejected.

Do not shudder at the thought that there can be no moral stability where there is such liberty. It was once believed that there could be no stable form of government except an absolute monarchy. It is now well established that an intelligent republic, where each citizen is a free political agent, is the strongest form of government in the world. So it will yet be found that the firmness and stability of a moral purpose are more reliable, more enduring than mountains of granite. These are the conditions, and the only conditions, under which the grandest character, the noblest, purest, most exalted virtue, can be attained and held unalterably through the ages of eternity.

When "the heavens shall pass away with a great noise, and the elements (heavenly bodies) shall be dissolved with fervent heat, and the earth and the works that are therein shall be burned up," and during all the ages that follow, the fixed purpose of every moral agent will be waxing stronger and stronger.

"The stars shall fade away, the sun himself
Grow dim with age, and nature sink in years;
But thou shall flourish in immortal youth,
Unhurt amidst the war of elements,
The wreck of matter, and the crush of worlds."

Should any poor, deluded sinner falsely and wickedly endeavor to use this doctrine as one of his "refuges of lies," with the idea that he will postpone repentance until he realizes the full consequences of sin in the future life, let him be assured that he who refuses the offers of Mercy, in this life, "who hath trodden under foot the Son of

God, and hath counted the blood of the covenant an unholy thing, and hath done despite unto the Spirit of grace," will have already reached his unalterable purpose, and sealed his own eternal doom. In regard to all such, no inducements can reach them in the regions of despair that they will not already, in this life, have spurned, scorned and defied. In their case, at least, there can be no doubt that every one will receive according to the deeds done in the body, whether they be good or bad. "Choose ye this day whom ye will serve."

www.ingramcontent.com/pod-product-compliance
Lightning Source LLC
Chambersburg PA
CBHW022026240426
43667CB00042B/1203